OPENING LEADS AND SIGNALS

Opening Leads and Signals

BY

JOHN MALLON

COLLIER BOOKS
A Division of Macmillan Publishing Co., Inc.
NEW YORK

COLLIER MACMILLAN PUBLISHERS
LONDON

Library of Congress
Catalog Card Number: 64-18207
First Collier Books Edition 1969

15   14   13   12   11   10   9   8   7   6   5

Opening Leads and Signals was first published
in a hardcover edition by Abelard-Schuman
and is reprinted by arrangement
Macmillan Publishing Co., Inc.
866 Third Avenue, New York, N.Y. 10022

Collier Macmillan Canada, Ltd.
Printed in the United States of America

FOREWORD

When your opponents have outbid you and secured the contract, good defensive play by you and your partner can frequently prevent your opponents from making their contract. You must choose the best opening lead available and also, during the play of the hand, you must exchange information with your partner, whenever possible, by means of certain conventional signals.

OPENING LEADS — The greatest weakness of the average bridge player is his opening lead. And yet no part of the game is more important. The choice of the opening lead, over and over again, determines whether the contract is made or set.

It is not necessary to memorize tables of leads or a lot of rules. There are only a few fundamental principles governing opening leads. These principles are based on common sense and the experience of generations of whist and bridge players. A player who understands these principles can select the best available lead from any hand.

SIGNALS — Although the defending partners can not see each other's hands, nevertheless, they can exchange a good deal of information about their hands by giving certain signals. These signals have been used so long and are so widely understood that they are now universally accepted conventions. They are really quite simple and easy to learn.

This book is offered as a text for learning or teaching the conventional leads and signals.

Every effort has been made to make this study as easy as possible. The principles and rules are condensed and simplified.

The material is logically arranged in 16 short lessons. In each lesson (because of the arrangement and contrasting size of the type) the essential instructions stand out and will stick in the reader's memory. Where bridge hands are shown they can be visualized without effort, because they look like cards picked up from the bridge table.

The first part of this book consists of 11 lessons covering opening leads.

The second part consists of 5 lessons covering the essential signals.

The third part consists of 24 quizzes illustrated by bridge hands with questions and answers on opening leads and signals.

The last part gives a short summary of the rules for leads and signals.

CONTENTS

OPENING LEADS

DEFINITIONS

IN SEQUENCE

Two cards are in sequence when they are in the same suit and in immediate consecutive order of value.

Examples. <u>K Q</u> 9, A <u>J 10</u> 3, Q <u>10 9</u> 6, <u>8 7</u> 4 2
The cards in sequence are underlined.

LEADABLE SEQUENCES

Certain combinations of high cards in the same suit are called Leadable Sequences.

There are 3 separate types of leadable sequences.

1. **Solid Sequence** — Three cards in sequence headed by an honor.
   Examples. A K Q, K Q J, Q J 10, J 10 9, 10 9 8.

2. **Interrupted Sequence** — Three cards headed by an honor, the 2 higher cards being in sequence, with a gap of 1 rank between the 2nd and 3rd card.
   Examples. A K J, K Q 10, Q J 9, J 10 8, 10 9 7.

3. **Intermediate Sequence** — Three cards, the middle card being an honor, the 2 lower cards being in sequence, with a gap of 1 or more ranks between the top card and the middle card.
   Examples. A Q J, A J 10, A 10 9, K J 10, K 10 9, Q 10 9.

TENACE

Any 2 cards in the same suit with a gap of 1 rank between them are called a tenace.

Examples. A Q, K J, Q 10, J 9, 10 8, 9 7, etc.

High Tenace — A Q and K J are called high tenaces. Q 10 is not considered a high tenace.

EXTRA TRUMPS

Small trumps which are not needed to protect a trump honor and which, therefore, can be used for ruffing without sacrificing the guard for the honor, are "extra" trumps.

Examples. A <u>3</u>, K 6 <u>4</u>, Q 8 4 <u>3</u>, <u>5 2</u>.
The "extra" trumps are underlined.

PART I

OPENING LEADS AT CONTRACT BRIDGE

The proper choice of an opening lead depends not only on the cards you hold and the type of contract (trump or No trump) which must be defeated, but also on information revealed by the bidding of your partner and your opponents.

In selecting an opening lead, you must make 2 decisions:
First decide: What suit to open.
Then decide: What card to lead from that suit.

Lessons 1 through 6 explain how to select the suit to open.
Lessons 7 through 10 explain how to select the card to lead from the suit you have chosen.

LESSON 1

THE SUIT TO LEAD AGAINST NO TRUMP
ATTACKING LEADS

When your opponents have outbid you and secured a No trump contract, they almost always hold a preponderance of the high cards. In this case the high cards in your hand and your partner's will not be sufficient to set the contract. To do so you must take additional tricks with some of your low cards.

As a general rule make an attacking lead by opening the suit which promises to be the longest and strongest suit in your hand and your partner's hand combined.
Save your high cards in other suits as entries to recapture the lead, until you finally establish this long suit and can take tricks with some of its low cards.

If your partner did not bid a suit of his own, **lead your own longest and strongest suit.**

If your partner did bid a suit, **usually lead your partner's suit, even though you have a long, strong suit of your own.**

However, you may decide to open your own suit instead of your partner's under any of the following conditions:
1. If your partner raised the suit you bid.
2. If you have a singleton in your partner's suit and a strong suit of your own.
3. If you have a long, strong suit and enough entries to defeat the contract without help from your partner.

Whenever you are not sure whether your own suit or your partner's suit is the longest and strongest in the combined hands, open your partner's suit.

ATTACKING LEADS

Lead longest and strongest suit in combined hands.

Prefer partner's suit to your own, unless you have:
1. Suit you bid and partner raised.
2. Singleton in partner's suit and a strong suit of your own.
3. Long solid suit and enough entries to set contract unaided.

LESSON 2

THE SUIT TO LEAD AGAINST NO TRUMP
PROTECTING LEADS

When your partner has not bid a suit of his own or raised a suit you have bid, frequently you have no good attacking lead available; because under any of the following conditions an opening lead from your own longest suit is not recommended, unless your partner has raised your suit.

a. *If your long suit is weak,* and you do not have enough entries in other suits to establish your long suit and then recapture the lead again. In this case the low cards in your suit will never take tricks.

b. *If your long suit was bid by declarer or dummy,* and it is not headed by a solid sequence.

c. *If your longest suit contains only 4 cards,* and it is headed by only 1 honor or by a high tenace.

Under any of the above conditions it is usually better to make a good protecting lead instead of leading from your longest suit.

The best protecting leads are those which are safe and will not increase the risk of losing a high card in your hand.
They can be made as follows.

1. Lead a worthless 4-card suit.
2. Lead a worthless 3-card suit.
   A 3-card suit headed J 10 or 10 9 is also recommended.

Protecting leads which are not desirable, but are acceptable if no better lead is available, can be made as follows.

1. Lead a 3-card suit headed by 2 honors in sequence.
   A K x, K Q x, and Q J x are in this class.
   Avoid a 3-card suit headed by only 1 honor or by 2 honors not in sequence.
2. Lead a low doubleton.
   Avoid a doubleton headed by an honor.

In choosing a protecting lead avoid any suit which was bid by either of your opponents — especially a suit bid by the declarer.

PROTECTING LEADS

Lead worthless 4-card suit.
Lead worthless 3-card suit.
Lead 3-card suit headed by 2 honors in sequence.
Lead low doubleton.

WHAT SUIT DO YOU LEAD?

1. **♠ Q 7 5 3 2 ♡ J 5 3 ♣ J 4 ◇ 8 5 2**

Opponents' contract is 3 No trump.
Your partner did not bid.

2. **♠ K J 10 8 2 ♡ 8 3 2 ♣ Q 7 3 ◇ A 4**

Opponents' contract is 3 No trump.
Your partner did not bid.
Declarer bid Spades.

ANSWERS

1. **Lead Diamonds.** Your hand is so weak that there is no hope of establishing your own long suit. So make a protecting short suit lead, instead of leading your longest suit. Against a No trump contract prefer a 3-card suit to a doubleton. Do not lead Hearts, because it is a 3-card suit headed by only 1 honor.

2. **Lead Hearts.** If your only long suit was bid by your opponents, and it is not headed by a solid sequence, make a protecting short suit lead. Do not lead Clubs, because your 3-card Club suit is headed by a single honor. Against a No trump contract a lead from a worthless 3-card suit is a good protecting lead.

WHAT SUIT DO YOU LEAD?

3.

| 7 5 3 | 8 2 | A Q 5 3 | A 8 4 2 |
| ♠ ♠ ♠ | ♡ ♡ | ♣ ♣ ♣ ♣ | ◇ ◇ ◇ ◇ |

Opponents' contract is 3 No trump.
Your partner did not bid.

4.

| 7 2 | K J 10 8 3 | K 8 5 | Q J 3 |
| ♠ ♠ | ♡ ♡ ♡ ♡ ♡ | ♣ ♣ ♣ | ◇ ◇ ◇ |

Opponents' contract is 3 No trump.
Your partner did not bid.
Declarer bid Hearts.

5.

| K J 4 3 | K 7 5 4 | 7 2 | K J 2 |
| ♠ ♠ ♠ ♠ | ♡ ♡ ♡ ♡ | ♣ ♣ | ◇ ◇ ◇ |

Opponents' contract is 3 No trump.
Your partner did not bid.

6.

| A Q 3 2 | 8 7 5 4 | 7 2 | K 8 5 |
| ♠ ♠ ♠ ♠ | ♡ ♡ ♡ ♡ | ♣ ♣ | ◇ ◇ ◇ |

Opponents' contract is 3 No trump.
Your partner did not bid.

7.

| A Q 3 2 | K 7 5 4 | 7 2 | J 10 5 |
| ♠ ♠ ♠ ♠ | ♡ ♡ ♡ ♡ | ♣ ♣ | ◇ ◇ ◇ |

Opponents' contract is 3 No trump.
Your partner did not bid.

ANSWERS

3. **Lead Spades.** If you have no suit longer than 4 cards, and your 4-card suit is headed by only 1 honor or by a high tenace, make a protecting short suit lead. Against a No trump contract lead from a worthless 3-card suit rather than from a doubleton.

4. **Lead Diamonds.** Although you have a long, strong Heart suit, do not lead it. Do not lead a suit which was bid by your opponents, unless it is headed by a solid sequence. Your 3-card Diamond suit headed by 2 honors in sequence does not offer a very desirable protecting lead. But a lead from your low doubleton in Spades is probably even less desirable against a No trump contract.

5. **Lead Clubs.** Here you have a choice of evils. Avoid leading from a 4-card suit headed by a single honor or by a high tenace. So do not lead Hearts or Spades. Avoid a 3-card suit headed by 2 honors not in sequence. So do not lead Diamonds. Against a No trump contract a lead from a doubleton is undesirable, but with this hand it is the least damaging lead you can make.

6. **Lead Hearts.** Your longest and strongest suit is Spades. However, it should not be led because it is a suit of only 4 cards headed by a high tenace. A good protecting lead can be made from your worthless 4-card Heart suit.

    If the Spade suit contained 5 cards headed by the A Q tenace, the proper lead would be Spades.

7. **Lead Diamonds.** You have no suit longer than 4 cards. Neither of your two 4-card suits should be led. One is headed by a high tenace, the other by only 1 honor. Make a protecting lead. A 3-card suit headed J 10 is a very good protecting lead.

WHAT SUIT DO YOU LEAD?

3.

| 8 5 2 | A Q 4 2 | 5 3 | K Q 10 7 |
| ♠ ♠ ♠ | ♡ ♡ ♡ ♡ | ♣ ♣ | ◇ ◇ ◇ ◇ |

Opponents' contract is 4 Spades.
Your partner did not bid.

4.

| Q 7 4 | A Q 5 3 | 6 5 | K J 10 5 |
| ♠ ♠ ♠ | ♡ ♡ ♡ ♡ | ♣ ♣ | ◇ ◇ ◇ ◇ |

Opponents' contract is 4 Spades.
You bid Hearts.
Your partner raised your Hearts.

5.

| K 8 7 | 8 4 3 | 7 5 3 | Q J 5 2 |
| ♠ ♠ ♠ | ♡ ♡ ♡ | ♣ ♣ ♣ | ◇ ◇ ◇ ◇ |

Opponents' contract is 4 Hearts.
Your partner bid Spades.

6.

| 9 7 5 3 | A Q 7 6 2 | K 4 2 | 8 |
| ♠ ♠ ♠ ♠ | ♡ ♡ ♡ ♡ ♡ | ♣ ♣ ♣ | ◇ |

Opponents' contract is 4 Spades.
Your partner did not bid.

7.

| J 7 2 | Q J 5 3 | 8 4 2 | Q 7 6 |
| ♠ ♠ ♠ | ♡ ♡ ♡ ♡ | ♣ ♣ ♣ | ◇ ◇ ◇ |

Opponents' contract is 4 Spades.
Dummy bid Clubs.
Your partner did not bid.

8.

| 6 | J 4 3 | Q J 10 2 | K Q 9 6 4 |
| ♠ | ♡ ♡ ♡ | ♣ ♣ ♣ ♣ | ◇ ◇ ◇ ◇ ◇ |

Opponents' contract is 2 Spades.
Your partner did not bid.

ANSWERS

3. **Lead Diamonds.** A 4-card or longer suit headed by an interrupted sequence offers a good attacking lead. Do not lead Hearts. Avoid leading a suit headed by a high tenace.

4. **Lead Hearts.** Do not hesitate to lead the suit you bid, if your partner raised it, no matter how your suit is headed. Do not lead Diamonds. Avoid leading a suit headed by an intermediate sequence.

5. **Lead Spades.** A good attacking lead is a lead from a suit which your partner bid, no matter how your holding in his suit is headed.

6. **Lead Hearts.** Against a trump contract, if you have 4 or more trumps, lead the suit you would normally open against a No trump contract. Against a No trump contract you would lead your longest and strongest suit. You would lead from your 5-card suit, even though it is headed by a high tenace.

   If you and your partner keep plugging away at the Heart suit, you may be able to force the declarer to trump 1 or 2 Hearts and make him exhaust his trumps by drawing your 4 Spades. If this can be done before you have to play your K of Clubs entry, you will be able to take tricks with your remaining Hearts.

7. **Lead Hearts.** A 4-card suit headed by 2 honors in sequence other than A K does not offer a desirable attacking lead. However, no other attacking lead is available.

8. **Lead Clubs.** A lead from a 4-card or longer suit headed by a solid sequence is a very good attacking lead. Do not lead Diamonds. A lead from a 4-card or longer suit headed by 2 honors in sequence other than A K should be made only if no better lead is available.

LESSON 5

THE SUIT TO LEAD AGAINST A TRUMP CONTRACT
RUFFING LEADS

Occasionally a good ruffing lead will help defeat a trump contract by enabling you to trump a trick before the declarer can draw your trumps.

The lead of a singleton *in your partner's suit* is always a good ruffing lead, if you hold "extra" trumps.

The lead of a singleton or a doubleton A K, *in a suit your partner did not bid,* is a good ruffing lead only when all the following conditions apply.

1. **Your partner has bid.**

Unless your partner has bid, indicating that he may have a quick entry in his suit, your trumps will almost surely be drawn before your partner can take a trick and lead back the suit you can trump.

2. **You hold a sure stopper in the trump suit.**

If your opponent takes the first trick and tries to draw your trumps, you must be able to stop the trump suit and lead to your partner's suit, while you still have a trump left with which you can ruff.

A trump stopper is not required if you lead a singleton A or a doubleton A K. After you have led out your singleton A or doubleton A K, you can lead your partner's suit before the declarer gets a chance to lead trumps.

3. **You hold at least 1 "extra" trump.**

You gain nothing if you ruff with a trump which you need to guard an honor.

When you hold 4 or more trumps, even though you have all the requirements for a good singleton lead, do not lead your singleton. Open the suit you would lead if the hand were being played against a No trump contract.

Try to establish a long suit and make the declarer trump it as often as you can. In this way you may be able to shorten his long trump suit, so that he may be compelled to use all of his remaining trumps to draw yours.

Then, if you still have an entry, you will be able to take tricks with your established low cards.

You usually gain more in this way than you would gain by ruffing.

REQUIREMENTS FOR RUFFING LEADS

Your partner has bid.
You hold a stopper in trumps.
You hold at least 1 extra trump.
You hold not more than 3 trumps.

WHAT SUIT DO YOU LEAD?

1.

A 8 6	7 5 3 2	A Q 5 4 2	2
♠ ♠ ♠	♡ ♡ ♡ ♡	♣ ♣ ♣ ♣ ♣	◇

Opponents' contract is 4 Spades.
Your partner bid Hearts.

2.

Q 8 6 4	7 5 3 2	J 10 5 4	2
♠ ♠ ♠ ♠	♡ ♡ ♡ ♡	♣ ♣ ♣ ♣	◇

Opponents' contract is 4 Spades.
Your partner bid Hearts.

ANSWERS

1. **Lead Diamonds.** You hold not more than 3 trumps, including 2 "extra" trumps. You have a stopper in trumps. Your partner has bid, indicating that he probably has an entry. Therefore, the lead of a singleton in a suit which was not bid by your partner is a good ruffing lead.

2. **Lead Hearts.** Do not lead your singleton Diamond, even though you have all the requirements for a good ruffing lead. If you have 4 or more trumps, lead the suit you would open against a No trump contract.

If you can establish your partner's Heart suit and force declarer to trump it often enough, you can cut down declarer's trump advantage. You may even end up with control of the trump suit. In that event, if your partner can get the lead again, he can take tricks with his low Hearts.

WHAT SUIT DO YOU LEAD?

3.

| Q 8 6 | 7 5 3 2 | K Q 5 4 2 | 2 |
| ♠ ♠ ♠ | ♡ ♡ ♡ ♡ | ♣ ♣ ♣ ♣ ♣ | ♢ |

Opponents' contract is 4 Spades.
Your partner bid Hearts.

4.

| K 8 6 | 7 5 3 2 | Q J 10 4 2 | 2 |
| ♠ ♠ ♠ | ♡ ♡ ♡ ♡ | ♣ ♣ ♣ ♣ ♣ | ♢ |

Opponents' contract is 4 Spades.
Your partner did not bid.

5.

| 8 6 4 | 7 5 3 2 | Q J 7 3 2 | A |
| ♠ ♠ ♠ | ♡ ♡ ♡ ♡ | ♣ ♣ ♣ ♣ ♣ | ♢ |

Opponents' contract is 4 Spades.
Your partner bid Hearts.

6.

| 8 6 4 | 7 5 3 | Q J 7 3 2 | A K |
| ♠ ♠ ♠ | ♡ ♡ ♡ | ♣ ♣ ♣ ♣ ♣ | ♢ ♢ |

Opponents' contract is 4 Spades.
Your partner bid Hearts.

7.

| Q 6 3 2 | A 7 6 | 5 | 8 6 5 3 2 |
| ♠ ♠ ♠ ♠ | ♡ ♡ ♡ | ♣ | ♢ ♢ ♢ ♢ ♢ |

Opponents' contract is 4 Hearts
Your partner bid Spades.

ANSWERS

3. **Lead Hearts.** A lead from the suit your partner bid is a good attacking lead. Do not lead the singleton Diamond. You need both of your small trumps to guard the Q. Therefore, you do not want to trump.

4. **Lead Clubs.** A good attacking lead can be made from a 4-card or longer suit headed by a solid sequence. The singleton Diamond is not a good ruffing lead, because your partner did not bid and you can not count on him for an entry. If you were to lead Diamonds, declarer would probably take the first trick and then extract your trumps before you would get a chance to ruff.

5. **Lead Diamonds.** You hold not more than 3 trumps, all of which are "extra" trumps. Your partner has bid, indicating that he has an entry. The lead of a singleton A is a good ruffing lead, when your partner has bid. A trump stopper is not required when you lead a singleton A.

6. **Lead Diamonds.** After you have cashed your A and K of Diamonds, you may be able to get into your partner's hand by leading his Heart suit. If so, he can return the Diamond suit, and you can ruff with an otherwise worthless trump. A doubleton A K is a good ruffing lead when your partner has bid, even when you do not have a stopper in the trump suit.

7. **Lead Clubs.** You have all the requirements for a good singleton lead. You have 2 trumps which are not required to guard an honor. You can stop the first round of trumps and lead your partner's suit before your trumps are drawn. Your partner has bid Spades, so he probably has a quick entry in that suit. If he can get in on the first lead of Spades, he will return a Club which you can trump.

LESSON 6

THE SUIT TO LEAD AGAINST A TRUMP CONTRACT
PROTECTING LEADS

If, as is often the case, your hand does not contain a good attacking lead or a good ruffing lead, the best opening lead is usually a protecting, or short suit lead.

The best protecting leads are leads which are safe and will not increase the risk of losing a high card in your hand.
They can be made as follows.

1. **Lead a low doubleton not headed by an honor.**
2. **Lead a worthless 3-card suit.**
A 3-card suit headed J 10 or 10 9 is also recommended.
3. **Lead a worthless 4-card suit.**

Protecting leads which are less desirable but still acceptable can be made as follows.

1. **Lead a 3-card suit headed by 2 honors in sequence.**
A K x, K Q x, and Q J x are in this classification.
J 10 x is one of the best protecting leads.
2. **Lead trumps, if you hold 2 or 3 low trumps.**
Avoid a trump lead if it would risk the loss of a trump honor in your hand.
Avoid a trump lead if you hold a singleton trump or if you hold 4 or more trumps.
If you hold 4 or more trumps, open the suit you would lead if the hand were being played against a No trump contract. If you can establish a long suit and force declarer to trump it often enough, you may end up in control of the trump suit instead of the declarer.
Whenever, because of the bidding, you suspect that dummy has a short side suit, a trump lead becomes one of the best protecting leads — almost a required lead. Lead trumps in order to remove dummy's trumps before the declarer can use them for ruffing.
A short side suit in the dummy is indicated:
1. When declarer has bid 2 suits, and dummy has raised 1 but has not supported the other.
2. When declarer jumps to game, after dummy has given a single raise to an opening bid of 1 in a suit.

Against a trump contract lead a low doubleton in preference to a worthless 3-card or a worthless 4-card suit.

In choosing a protecting lead avoid any side suit which was bid by the declarer.

PROTECTING LEADS

Lead low doubleton.
Lead worthless 3-card suit.
Lead worthless 4-card suit.
Lead 3-card suit headed by 2 honors in sequence.
Lead trumps, if you hold 2 or 3 small trumps only.

WHAT SUIT DO YOU LEAD?

Opponents' contract is 4 Hearts.
Your partner did not bid.

Opponents' contract is 4 hearts.
Your partner did not bid.

ANSWERS

Lead Diamonds. No good attacking lead is available. Avoid a 4-card suit headed by only 1 honor. A lead from a worthless 4-card suit is a very good protecting lead. Do not lead from the doubleton in Spades, because it is headed by an honor. Do not lead trumps. A trump lead might result in the loss of your K.

Lead Clubs. You have no good attacking lead. A 4-card or a 5-card suit headed by only one honor should be avoided. A lead from a worthless 3-card suit is a very good protecting lead. Do not lead trumps. A singleton trump is a very poor lead.

WHAT SUIT DO YOU LEAD?

3.
| 8 5 | K 9 7 | K 7 4 2 | 7 6 5 3 |
| ♠ ♠ | ♡ ♡ ♡ | ♣ ♣ ♣ ♣ | ◇ ◇ ◇ ◇ |

Opponents' contract is 4 Hearts.
Your partner did not bid.

4.
| J 5 | 9 7 4 | K 7 4 2 | Q 6 5 3 |
| ♠ ♠ | ♡ ♡ ♡ | ♣ ♣ ♣ ♣ | ◇ ◇ ◇ ◇ |

Opponents' contract is 4 Hearts.
Your partner did not bid.

5.
| Q 5 | 9 7 4 2 | J 10 9 8 | 8 6 5 |
| ♠ ♠ | ♡ ♡ ♡ ♡ | ♣ ♣ ♣ ♣ | ◇ ◇ ◇ |

Opponents' contract is 4 Hearts.
Your partner did not bid.

6.
| Q J 5 | K 8 | 8 7 4 3 2 | A J 2 |
| ♠ ♠ ♠ | ♡ ♡ | ♣ ♣ ♣ ♣ ♣ | ◇ ◇ ◇ |

Opponents' contract is 4 Hearts.
Your partner did not bid.

7.
| Q 5 | K 9 7 | K 7 4 2 | Q 6 5 3 |
| ♠ ♠ | ♡ ♡ ♡ | ♣ ♣ ♣ ♣ | ◇ ◇ ◇ ◇ |

Opponents' contract is 4 Hearts.
Your partner did not bid.
Declarer bid both Hearts and Spades.
Dummy raised declarer's Hearts.

ANSWERS

3. **Lead Spades.** You do not have a good attacking lead. A Club lead would give your adversary a chance to pick up an extra Club trick. A lead from a low doubleton is a very good protecting lead against a trump contract. The Spade lead is not only safe, but also gives you a remote chance for a ruff. Do not lead Hearts. A trump lead is desirable only when you hold 2 or 3 small trumps only.

4. **Lead Hearts.** Make a protecting lead, because you have no good attacking lead. Avoid a 4-card suit headed by only 1 honor. A lead of trumps is an acceptable protecting lead when you have 2 or 3 small trumps only. Do not lead from the doubleton Spade, because it is headed by an honor.

5. **Lead Clubs.** Do not lead trumps, because you have more than 3 trumps. Do not lead Diamonds, even though it is a very good protecting lead. Whenever you hold 4 or more trumps, do not make a protecting lead. Lead the suit you would open against a No trump contract.

6. **Lead Spades.** Your worthless 5-card Club suit is not a good attacking lead. A 3-card suit headed by 2 honors in sequence, although not a desirable protecting lead, is still acceptable when no better lead is available. Do not lead Diamonds. Avoid a 3-card suit headed by 2 honors not in sequence. Do not lead trumps. Avoid a trump lead if you hold a trump honor.

7. **Lead Clubs.** Your Spade suit is a very poor protecting lead, because the doubleton is headed by an honor, and also because declarer bid that suit. A trump lead from K x x is very undesirable, so do not lead Hearts.

   You have a better chance to establish a trick in Clubs than in Diamonds. So lead Clubs, even though a lead from a 4-card suit headed by only 1 honor is a poor attacking lead.

LESSON 7

THE CARD TO LEAD
WHEN LEADING AN HONOR

When you hold 2 or more honors which are in sequence,° *if you lead one of the touching honors,* lead the highest of the equal or touching honors.

Exception. From a 3-card or longer suit headed A K, lead the K instead of the A.

This exception does not apply when you lead from a very long solid or almost solid suit against a No trump contract. Lead the A if you hold:
4-card or 5-card suit headed A K Q J.
6-card suit headed A K Q; or A K J 10 or A Q J 10 with an entry.
7-card suit headed A K J or A K 10; or A Q J with an entry.

When you lead an A against a No trump contract, you tell your partner to "unblock" by throwing away his highest card each time the suit is led.

From a *solid sequence*°° or an *interrupted sequence*°°° lead the highest honor in the sequence.

Exception. If your suit is headed A K, lead the K.

From an *intermediate sequence*°°°° lead the middle card, that is, the higher of the 2 touching or equal cards.

Exception. If your intermediate sequence is headed by the A you lead the A against a trump contract.

From a suit headed by *2 honors in sequence,*° with only 2 honors in the suit, lead the higher of the equal honors.

Exceptions. 1. If your suit is headed A K, lead the K.

2. Sometimes you lead fourth best against No trump

The conditions under which you lead fourth best, instead of the higher of the 2 touching honors, will be explained in Lesson 10.

° In Sequence — Two cards are in sequence when they are in the same suit and in immediate consecutive order of value.

°° Solid Sequence
A K Q, K Q J, Q J 10, J 10 9, 10 9 8.

°°° Interrupted Sequence
A K J, K Q 10, Q J 9, J 10 8, 10 9 7.

°°°°Intermediate Sequence
A Q J, A J 10, A 10 9, K J 10, K 10 9, Q 10 9.

WHEN LEADING AN HONOR

From touching honors lead highest honor in sequence.
Exception   Lead K from suit headed A K.

WHICH HONOR CARD DO YOU LEAD?

A <u>K</u> x x,   <u>K</u> Q x x,   <u>Q</u> J x x,   <u>J</u> 10 x x,   <u>10</u> 9 x x*

If you lead an honor from a suit headed by 2 honors in sequence, lead the higher of the 2 equal or touching honors, unless the suit is headed A K.

Conditions under which you lead fourth best instead of leading an honor will be explained in Lesson 10.

A <u>K</u> Q x,   <u>K</u> Q J x,   <u>Q</u> J 10 x,   <u>J</u> 10 9 x,   <u>10</u> 9 8 x*
A <u>K</u> J x,   <u>K</u> Q 10 x,   <u>Q</u> J 9 x,   <u>J</u> 10 9 x*

From a solid sequence or an interrupted sequence always lead the highest honor, unless the suit is headed A K.

K <u>J</u> 10 x,   K <u>10</u> 9 x,   Q <u>10</u> 9 x*

From an intermediate sequence not headed by the A, always lead the middle card in the sequence.

A Q J x,   A J 10 x,   A 10 9 x*

From an intermediate sequence headed by the A,
Against a No trump contract lead the middle card.
Against a trump contract lead the A

* Note — 10 9 x is treated as though the 9 were an honor.

LESSON 8

THE CARD TO LEAD
FROM A DOUBLETON

From any doubleton always lead the higher of the 2 cards.
This rule applies even to a doubleton A K.

Examples   <u>A</u> K,   <u>K</u> Q,   <u>K</u> x,   <u>Q</u> x,   <u>J</u> x,   <u>10</u> x,   <u>7</u> 6,   etc.
The card to lead is underlined.

LESSON 9

THE CARD TO LEAD
FROM A 3-CARD SUIT

As a general rule when you lead from a suit of 3 cards, lead the highest card in the suit.

From a worthless 3-card suit always lead the highest card.°
Examples   9 8 7,   7 5 3,   6 3 2 — Lead the highest card.

From a 3-card suit in which the 2 top cards are equal or touching honors, lead the highest card in the suit.
Exception. If the suit is headed A K, lead the K.

Examples   K Q J,   K Q 10,   Q J x,   10 9 x — Lead highest card.
Note — 10 9 x is treated as if the 9 were an honor.
A K Q,   A K J,   A K 10,   A K x — Lead the K.

From a 3-card suit containing only 1 honor or 2 honors not in sequence, lead the lowest card in the suit.
Exception. When you hold the A, lead the A if the hand is being played against a trump contract.

K x x,   10 x x,   K J x,   Q 10 x—Lead lowest card.

Examples   A x x, A Q x, A J x, A 10 x—Lead lowest card against
a No trump contract. Lead A against trump contract.

From a 3-card suit consisting of an intermediate sequence, lead the middle card (i.e., the higher of the 2 touching cards in the sequence).
Exception. When you hold the A, lead the A if the hand is being played against a trump contract.

K J 10,   K 10 9,   Q 10 9—Lead the middle card.

A J 10,   A 10 9—Lead the middle card against
a No trump contract. Lead A against trump contract.
Examples

A Q J—This is a special case—Always lead the A.

° Some top-ranking players prefer to lead the lowest card from a worthless 3-card suit. But the conventional practice is to lead "top of nothing." So lead your highest card unless, before the game starts, your partner requests you to lead low from a worthless 3-card suit.

FROM 3-CARD SUIT

Worthless Suit
Lead highest card.

Suit headed 2 or more honors in sequence
Lead highest card.
Exception Lead K from suit headed A K.

Suit headed 1 honor or 2 honors not in sequence
Lead lowest card.
Exception Lead A against trump contract.

Suit headed by intermediate sequence
Lead middle card.
Exception Lead A against trump contract.

WHAT CARD DO YOU LEAD?

1. **9 7 3 ♠ ♠ ♠** Opponents' contract is 4 Hearts.
Your partner did not bid.

2. **Q J 2 ♡ ♡ ♡** Opponents' contract is 3 No trump.
Your partner bid Hearts.

3. **A K 4 ◇ ◇ ◇** Opponents' contract is 4 Hearts.
Your partner did not bid.

ANSWERS

1. **Lead the 9.** Lead the highest card from a worthless 3-card suit, unless your partner has requested you to lead low.

2. **Lead the Q.** When you lead from a 3-card suit headed by 2 honors in sequence, lead the highest card in the suit unless the suit is headed A K.

3. **Lead the K.** From a 3-card suit headed A K, always lead the K instead of the A.

WHAT CARD DO YOU LEAD?

4. 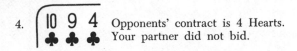 Opponents' contract is 4 Hearts.
    Your partner did not bid.

5. 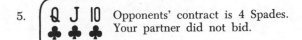 Opponents' contract is 4 Spades.
    Your partner did not bid.

6. 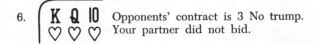 Opponents' contract is 3 No trump.
    Your partner did not bid.

7. 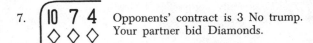 Opponents' contract is 3 No trump.
    Your partner bid Diamonds.

8. 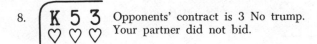 Opponents' contract is 3 No trump.
    Your partner did not bid.

9. 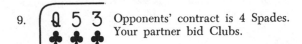 Opponents' contract is 4 Spades.
    Your partner bid Clubs.

10. 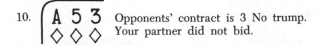 Opponents' contract is 3 No trump.
    Your partner did not bid.

11. 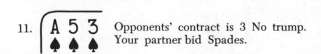 Opponents' contract is 3 No trump.
    Your partner bid Spades.

12. **A 5 3**
♡ ♡ ♡   Opponents' contract is 4 Spades.
Your partner did not bid.

ANSWERS

4. **Lead the 10.** In a 3-card suit the 10 9 sequence is treated like 2 honors in sequence. Lead the highest card in the suit.

5. **Lead the Q.** In any solid sequence, of course, the two highest cards are always honors in sequence. So lead the highest card in the suit, unless the 2 top cards are the A and K.

6. **Lead the K.** An interrupted sequence is always headed by 2 touching honors. So lead the highest card in the suit unless it is headed A K.

7. **Lead the 4.** This is not considered a worthless 3-card suit, because it is headed by the 10 which is an honor. Lead the lowest card from a 3-card suit headed by just one honor.

8. **Lead the 3.** When you lead from a 3-card suit headed by only 1 honor, always lead the lowest card against a No trump contract.

9. **Lead the 3.** Always lead low from K x x, Q x x, J x x, or 10 x x.

10. **Lead the 3.** Against a No trump contract, always lead low from a 3-card suit headed by a single honor. There are no exceptions to this rule.

11. **Lead the 3.** From A x x lead the lowest card against a No trump contract, even when you lead your partner's suit.

12. **Lead the A.** Against a suit contract when you lead from A x x lead the A.

LESSON 10

THE CARD TO LEAD
FROM A SUIT OF 4 CARDS OR LONGER

As a general rule, when you lead from a suit of 4 cards or longer, lead the fourth best card in the suit.

However, this is not a hard and fast rule. Frequently you are required to lead an honor instead of the fourth highest card in the suit. The decision whether or not to lead an honor is influenced by all the following considerations: (a) What high cards you hold; (b) Whether the contract is trump or No trump; (c) Whether or not your partner bid the suit.

Lead an honor instead of fourth best in any of the situations described below.

AGAINST A TRUMP CONTRACT

When you lead from any suit (partner's suit or any other suit)

Lead an honor if you hold the A, or 2 honors in sequence, or a leadable sequence.

1. When the suit is headed by the A, with or without other honors, lead the A.°
2. When the suit is headed by only 2 honors in sequence, lead the higher of the 2 touching honors.°
3. When the suit is headed by a leadable sequence, lead the highest of the equal or touching cards in the sequence.°

AGAINST A NO TRUMP CONTRACT

When you lead from a suit which was bid by your partner

Lead an honor if you hold 2 honors in sequence or a leadable sequence.

1. When the suit is headed by only 2 honors in sequence, lead the higher of the 2 touching honors.°
2. When the suit is headed by a leadable sequence, lead the highest of the equal or touching cards in the sequence.°

When you lead from a suit which was not bid by your partner

Lead an honor only if you hold a leadable sequence.

1. When the suit is headed by a leadable sequence, lead the highest of the equal or touching cards in the sequence.°

°*Exception* If you lead an honor from a suit headed A K, lead the K.

FROM 4-CARD OR LONGER SUIT

Lead fourth best, as a general rule.

Lead an honor instead of fourth best from the following suits:

Against trump contract
Any suit headed A, or 2 honors in sequence, or a leadable sequence.

Against No trump
Partner's suit headed 2 honors in sequence, or a leadable sequence.
Suit not partner's headed .... a leadable sequence.

WHAT CARD DO YOU LEAD?

1. **9 8 7 6** ♠ ♠ ♠ ♠ Opponents' contract is 4 Hearts.
Your partner did not bid.

2. **Q 9 6 2** ♡ ♡ ♡ ♡ Opponents' contract is 3 No trump.
Your partner bid Hearts.

ANSWERS

1. **Lead the 6.** Whenever you lead from a 4-card or longer suit which contains no honor cards, always lead fourth best. If you were to lead any other card, your partner would probably mistake it for the top of a worthless 3-card suit or a doubleton.

2. **Lead the 2.** Always lead fourth best from a 4-card or longer suit if the suit is headed by the K, Q, J, or 10, and there is no other honor in the suit. This is the proper lead from such a suit no matter what the contract is, and regardless of whether your partner did or did not bid the suit.

WHAT CARD DO YOU LEAD?

3. K J 7 3 2
   ♣ ♣ ♣ ♣ ♣

Opponents' contract is 4 Hearts.
Your partner did not bid.

4. A 7 5 3 2
   ♦ ♦ ♦ ♦ ♦

Opponents' contract is 4 Spades.
Your partner did not bid.

5. A 7 5 3
   ♣ ♣ ♣ ♣

Opponents' contract is 3 No trump.
Your partner bid Clubs.

6. A K 5 4 3
   ♦ ♦ ♦ ♦ ♦

Opponents' contract is 4 Spades.
Your partner did not bid.

7. A K 5 4 2
   ♣ ♣ ♣ ♣ ♣

Opponents' contract is 3 No trump.
Your partner did not bid.

8. J 10 5 4
   ♡ ♡ ♡ ♡

Opponents' contract is 3 No trump.
Your partner bid Hearts.

9. Q J 7 6
   ♠ ♠ ♠ ♠

Opponents' contract is 4 Hearts.
Your partner did not bid.

10. K Q 8 5
    ♦ ♦ ♦ ♦

Opponents' contract is 3 No trump.
Your partner did not bid.

ANSWERS

3. **Lead the 3.** When you lead from a 4-card or longer suit headed K J, K 10, or Q 10, always lead fourth best.

4. **Lead the A.** Against a trump contract do not lead fourth best from a 4-card or longer suit headed by the A. Play the A on your opening lead, as it may be trumped if you hold it until a later round.

5. **Lead the 3.** When you hold the A x x x, lead fourth best against a No trump contract, even when you lead your partner's suit. Save the A to capture one of the high cards which declarer holds in that suit.

6. **Lead the K.** When your suit is headed by the A K, do not lead fourth best against a trump contract. Lead off with the K and take a free look at the dummy.

7. **Lead the 4.** Against a No trump contract when you lead a suit your partner did not bid, always lead fourth best unless you have a leadable sequence. When you lead fourth best, you will almost surely lose the first trick. But if your partner can eventually return your suit, the chances are that your A and K will draw the remaining Clubs, and you will take tricks with your 5 and 2 also.

8. **Lead the J.** Never lead fourth best if you hold 2 touching honors in your partner's suit. Your partner probably holds more Hearts than you do. Sacrifice your own high cards to establish your partner's suit.

9. **Lead the Q.** If you hold 2 honors in sequence, always lead high against a trump contract. Lead high regardless of whether your partner did or did not bid the suit you lead. Lead the higher of the 2 equal honors.

10. **Lead the 5.** If you hold 2 honors in sequence, against a No trump contract lead fourth best, unless the suit was bid by your partner.

WHAT CARD DO YOU LEAD?

11. Q J 10 6
     ◇ ◇ ◇ ◇

Opponents' contract is 4 Spades.
Your partner did not bid.

12. K Q 10 5
     ♣ ♣ ♣ ♣

Opponents' contract is 4 Hearts.
Your partner did not bid.

13. Q J 9 2
     ◇ ◇ ◇ ◇

Opponents' contract is 3 No trump.
Your partner did not bid.

14. Q 10 9 4
     ♣ ♣ ♣ ♣

Opponents' contract is 4 Spades.
Your partner did not bid.

15. A Q J 3
     ◇ ◇ ◇ ◇

Opponents' contract is 4 Spades.
Your partner did not bid.

16. A J 10 6
     ♠ ♠ ♠ ♠

Opponents' contract is 3 No trump.
Your partner did not bid.

17. A 10 9 5
     ♠ ♠ ♠ ♠

Opponents' contract is 3 No trump.
Your partner bid Spades.

ANSWERS

11. **Lead the Q.** Here you have a leadable sequence. Do not lead fourth best. Lead the top honor, if you hold a solid sequence.

12. **Lead the K.** When you hold an interrupted sequence, lead the top honor. Your K will drive out the A. If your partner can get the lead and return your suit, there is a good chance that both your Q and 10 will take tricks.

13. **Lead the Q.** Here again you have an interrupted sequence. Do not lead fourth best when you hold a leadable sequence. If you were to lead the 2, you might lose the first trick to the 10.

14. **Lead the 10.** This suit is headed by an intermediate sequence. Do not lead fourth best. Open with the highest honor in sequence (i.e., the highest of the 2 touching honors).

15. **Lead the A.** You hold an intermediate sequence. But in this case do not lead the Q, which is the highest honor in sequence, because your suit is headed by the A and the hand is being played at a trump contract.

16. **Lead the J.** Do not lead fourth best, because you have an intermediate sequence. Against a No trump contract, do not lead the A. Lead the J, which is the highest honor in sequence.

17. **Lead the 10.** In spite of the fact that you hold the A in your partner's suit, do not lead the A. When you lead from a suit containing a leadable sequence against a No trump contract, always lead the highest of the equal or touching cards in the sequence.

LESSON 11

LEADS AGAINST SLAM CONTRACT

Three considerations make the choice of an opening lead against a slam contract a somewhat different problem from the choice of an opening lead against a mere game contract.

1. Only 1 trick is required to set a grand slam and 2 to set a small slam.
2. Usually the only tricks you will take will be with high cards the first or second time a suit is led.
3. Your opening lead will usually be your only opportunity to make a preliminary play which will put a high card of your own in position to take a trick when the suit is led a second time.

Nevertheless, all the instructions in the previous lessons apply to opening leads against slams, as well as to leads against normal game contracts, except for Lessons 1 and 4, which deal with attacking leads from 4-card and longer suits.

Against a slam it is usually futile to try to establish a long suit. So conventional leads from long suits should be avoided, unless the lead is from a sequence which will establish immediately a card which will take a trick on the second lead of the suit.

Frequently the suit you should select for your opening lead is not the suit you would open against a mere game contract.

However, the card you should lead from any suit you open is usually the same against a slam or against a game contract.

LEADS AGAINST SMALL SLAMS

ATTACKING LEADS

When your opponents have stopped at a small slam, usually they must lose 1 trick, either when declarer draws trumps or when he establishes some other suit.

When you hold an A or a trump honor with which you expect to take a trick (or if you think that your partner does), your opening lead should be used, if possible, to establish immediately a second round winning card in some other suit.

Then if you or your partner can recapture the lead, the established card can be cashed and the contract set.

Since 1 trick alone will not set a small slam, an A should seldom be led, especially against a No trump slam. It should usually be held back for a reentry.

However, against a trump contract, if either you or your partner has a probable stopper in trumps or in some other suit declarer must establish, then the A should be led to avoid the risk of its being trumped later in the play of the hand.

PROTECTING LEADS

To establish an honor as a second round winner it is necessary to sacrifice another touching honor. But a high card should not be sacrificed in this way, especially against a No trump slam, unless you are reasonably confident that you have (or your partner has) the necessary reentry in another suit. If there is no prospect of such a reentry, make a protecting lead.

A protecting lead is also recommended when you have no apparent opportunity to establish a second round winner by your opening lead.

In choosing a protecting lead, a trump lead should usually be avoided.

A lead from some other worthless suit in your own hand stands a bare chance of establishing a winning card in your partner's hand. But a trump lead deliberately sacrifices the advantage of the opening lead and gives declarer the opportunity to draw trumps and to start establishing a side suit, before you have attempted to build up a trick.

DESPERATION LEADS

Against a trump contract when the situation is apparently hopeless, sometimes a desperation lead is worth a gamble.

A singleton may be led, even though you do not have the requirements for a good ruffing lead. It is led with the faint hope that your partner will have the A and return the lead immediately for you to trump.

With a lucky break a low lead from a suit headed by a lone K, or even a Q, may find another of the top honors in your partner's hand. If it does, this lead will set the contract or at least promote the K or Q to first place.

Such a desperation lead should not be made against 6 No trump; because any well guarded honor may eventually become a winner, if you can hold out against declarer's attack in that suit, or if declarer must try a finesse to establish the suit.

LEADS AGAINST GRAND SLAMS

ATTACKING LEADS

Your opponents will almost never bid a grand slam without first and second round control of all suits.

Consequently the opportunity to make an attacking lead that will establish a second round winner is seldom presented.

When you hold an A against a grand slam in a suit contract careful consideration should be given before leading it, because it will almost surely be trumped.

DESPERATION LEADS

A desperation lead is a poor gamble against a grand slam, because it will succeed only when your partner holds one of the top honors in the suit. This is too much to expect against a grand slam contract.

PROTECTING LEADS

A protecting lead is almost always the best against a grand slam.

WHEN PARTNER DOUBLES A SLAM CONTRACT

The instructions under this heading should be followed only when your partner and your opponents are advanced players.

Since good players do not recklessly go beyond game to bid a slam, you can not hope to set a slam by more than 1 trick.

A doubled slam, down 1, will net you an additional score of 50 points (not vulnerable) or 100 points (vulnerable).

But if your opponents redouble (which they are apt to do) and make their contract, they will net an additional 620 points at No trump, 590 in a major, or 410 in a minor suit.

Because by doubling you may lose so much more than you can gain, the double of a slam is not used to gain penalty points. It is used only to give a lead-directing signal, calling for an un-natural lead which will probably defeat the contract.

AGAINST A SLAM IN A TRUMP CONTRACT

When your partner doubles a slam contract, do not lead as you normally would.
Do not lead a suit you have bid.
Do not lead a suit your partner has bid.
Do not lead trumps.

When dummy has bid a suit of his own
Lead dummy's suit. If dummy has bid 2 suits, lead the suit he bid first. Your partner probably sits over a tenace in the dummy.

When dummy has not bid a side suit, but declarer has
Lead declarer's side suit. Your partner can probably trump it.

When neither declarer nor dummy has bid a side suit
Lead an unbid suit. Your partner probably has a void suit.

AGAINST A SLAM IN A NO TRUMP CONTRACT

A lead-directing double against a No trump contract is almost never used except to call for a lead through dummy's first bid suit.

LEADS AGAINST SLAMS

Attacking leads
Lead an A, or lead to establish a second round winner,
    but only with a probable re-entry in your own or partner's hand.
Avoid attacking leads against 6 No trump or any grand slam.

Protecting leads
Lead same as against mere game contract.
Usually avoid a trump lead.

Desperation leads
Lead a singleton, even without requirements for good ruffing lead.
Lead low from a suit containing a lone K or Q.
Avoid a desperation lead against 6 No trump or any grand slam.

When partner doubles a slam contract
Make an unusual lead.

WHAT IS YOUR OPENING LEAD?

1.

| A 5 | K 7 3 | 9 8 7 5 | 8 6 3 2 |
| ♠ ♠ | ♡ ♡ ♡ | ♣ ♣ ♣ ♣ | ◇ ◇ ◇ ◇ |

Opponents' contract is 6 Hearts.
Neither you nor your partner bid.
Dummy bid and rebid Diamonds.
You are West. The bidding was as follows:

SOUTH	WEST	NORTH	EAST
2 Hearts	Pass	3 Diamonds	Pass
3 Hearts	Pass	4 Diamonds	Pass
6 Hearts	Pass	Pass	Pass

2.

| A 6 2 | 7 4 3 | K Q 9 5 | 8 6 5 |
| ♠ ♠ ♠ | ♡ ♡ ♡ | ♣ ♣ ♣ ♣ | ◇ ◇ ◇ |

Opponents' contract is 6 Hearts.
Neither your nor your partner bid.
Dummy did not bid a suit of his own.
You are West. The bidding was as follows:

SOUTH	WEST	NORTH	EAST
2 Hearts	Pass	3 Hearts	Pass
4 No trump	Pass	5 Diamonds	Pass
6 Hearts	Pass	Pass	Pass

3.

| A 7 3 2 | 6 5 4 | 8 7 6 3 | Q 2 |
| ♠ ♠ ♠ ♠ | ♡ ♡ ♡ | ♣ ♣ ♣ ♣ | ◇ ◇ |

Opponents' contract is 6 Hearts
Your partner bid Diamonds
Dummy bid Clubs.
You are West. The bidding was as follows:

NORTH	EAST	SOUTH	WEST
1 Club	1 Diamond	2 Hearts	Pass
3 Hearts	Pass	6 Hearts	Pass
Pass	Pass		

4.
7 2	A 9 5	10 9 7 2	9 8 6 3
♠ ♠	♡ ♡ ♡	♣ ♣ ♣ ♣	◇ ◇ ◇ ◇

Opponents' contract is 6 No trump.
Your partner did not bid.
No suit was bid by declarer or dummy.
You are West. The bidding was as follows:

SOUTH	WEST	NORTH	EAST
1 No trump	Pass	4 No trump	Pass
6 No trump	Pass	Pass	Pass

ANSWERS

1. **Lead A of Spades.** Since dummy did not support declarer's Hearts, you can expect to take a trick with your K of Hearts. Dummy obviously has 5 or 6 Diamonds, and you have 4 Diamonds. So declarer may well be short in the Diamond suit. Therefore, lead out your A of Spades before declarer can discard Spades on dummy's Diamonds. You can count on your K of Hearts to take the setting trick.

2. **Lead K of Clubs.** It takes 2 tricks to set the contract. So do not lead your A of Spades. Save your A for a reentry. If you lead your K of Clubs, your Q will be in a position to take a trick when you recapture the lead with your A of Spades.

3. **Lead Q of Diamonds.** Do not lead your A of Spades. Lead your Q of Diamonds. This should build up a trick in your partner's hand. Then, if you can capture the lead with your A of Spades, you can lead another Diamond which your partner will take.

4. **Lead 10 of Clubs.** Probably the only trick you can take is the A of Hearts. But 1 trick is not enough to set the contract, so do not lead out your A. The best hope for a second trick is in Clubs.

WHAT IS YOUR OPENING LEAD?

1.
| A 9 2 | 9 7 5 | 9 7 5 | J 9 6 4 |
| ♠ ♠ ♠ | ♡ ♡ ♡ | ♣ ♣ ♣ | ◇ ◇ ◇ ◇ |

Opponents' contract is 6 Hearts.
Your partner did not bid.
Dummy bid Diamonds.
You are West. The bidding was as follows:

NORTH	EAST	SOUTH	WEST
1 Diamond	Pass	1 Heart	Pass
2 No trump	Pass	3 Hearts	Pass
6 Hearts	Pass	Pass	Pass

2.
| 10 7 4 | 9 7 5 4 2 | 10 6 5 3 | 8 |
| ♠ ♠ ♠ | ♡ ♡ ♡ ♡ ♡ | ♣ ♣ ♣ ♣ | ◇ |

Opponents' contract is 6 Spades.
Your partner did not bid.
Dummy bid Clubs.
You are West. The bidding was as follows:

SOUTH	WEST	NORTH	EAST
2 Spades	Pass	3 Hearts	Pass
3 Spades	Pass	4 Spades	Pass
4 No trump	Pass	5 Clubs	Pass
6 Spades	Pass	Pass	Pass

3.
| 9 7 5 | K 7 3 2 | 5 4 2 | 7 4 3 |
| ♠ ♠ ♠ | ♡ ♡ ♡ ♡ | ♣ ♣ ♣ | ◇ ◇ ◇ |

Opponents' contract is 6 Diamonds.
Your partner did not bid.
Dummy bid Spades.
You are West. The bidding was as follows:

NORTH	EAST	SOUTH	WEST
1 Spade	Pass	2 Diamonds	Pass
4 Diamonds	Pass	4 Spades	Pass
6 Diamonds	Pass	Pass	Pass

9 8 2	Q 3 2	10 9 7 5 4	4 3
♠ ♠ ♠	♡ ♡ ♡	♣ ♣ ♣ ♣ ♣	◇ ◇

4.

Opponents' contract is 6 Hearts.
Your partner doubled.
Your partner did not bid a suit.
Dummy bid Spades and Clubs.
You are West. The bidding was as follows:

NORTH	EAST	SOUTH	WEST
1 Spade	Pass	3 Hearts	Pass
4 Clubs	Pass	4 Hearts	Pass
5 Hearts	Pass	6 Hearts	Pass
Pass	Double	Pass	Pass
Pass			

ANSWERS

1. **Lead 9 of Clubs.** Do not lead Hearts. Against a slam usually avoid a trump lead. Do not lead your A of Spades. Your only chance to set this contract is to make a lead which will set up a trick in your partner's hand. With a lucky break a Club lead might find the A of Clubs in dummy and the K in your partner's hand.

2. **Lead 8 of Diamonds.** Your partner probably holds 1 winning card. If he happens to hold the A of Diamonds or a quick trump stopper so he can lead back Diamonds before your trumps are drawn, then this desperation lead will set the contract.

3. **Lead 2 of Hearts.** This is a desperation lead, made with the hope that the A or Q of Hearts is in your partner's hand. If you are lucky enough to find the A there, your partner will return the lead and your K will take the second trick. If the Q is in your partner's hand, your K will be ready to take a trick in case your partner can get the lead.

4. **Lead 9 of Spades.** Your partner's double is a lead-directing signal. It asks you to lead through the suit dummy bid first. Your partner probably holds a high tenace behind dummy's Spades with which he can take a trick. Your Q of Hearts will stand up if declarer holds both the A and K of trumps.

WHAT IS YOUR OPENING LEAD?

1. | 8 6 3 ♠ ♠ ♠ | 10 8 7 4 3 ♡ ♡ ♡ ♡ ♡ | 8 7 5 4 ♣ ♣ ♣ ♣ | 8 ♢ |

Opponents' contract is 6 Clubs.

Your partner doubled.

Your partner bid Diamonds.

Dummy did not bid a suit of his own.

Declarer bid Clubs and Hearts.

You are West. The bidding was as follows:

SOUTH	WEST	NORTH	EAST
1 Club	Pass	3 Clubs	3 Diamonds
3 Hearts	Pass	4 Clubs	Pass
6 Clubs	Pass	Pass	Double
Pass	Pass	Pass	

2. | K Q 10 9 8 2 ♠ ♠ ♠ ♠ ♠ ♠ | 8 4 2 ♡ ♡ ♡ | 8 7 6 ♣ ♣ ♣ | 8 ♢ |

Opponents' contract is 6 Hearts.

Your partner doubled.

Your partner did not bid a suit.

You bid Spades.

You are West. The bidding was as follows:

SOUTH	WEST	NORTH	EAST
1 Heart	1 Spade	3 Hearts	Pass
6 Hearts	Pass	Pass	Double
Pass	Pass	Pass	

ANSWERS

1. **Lead 4 of Hearts.** Your partner's double is a lead-directing signal. It asks you to lead declarer's side suit. Your partner is probably void in Hearts. Do not lead your partner's Diamonds and do not lead trumps.

2. **Lead 8 of Diamonds.** Do not lead your Spade suit. Your partner's double calls for the lead of one of the unbid suits. The distribution is obviously very uneven. Your partner may have a long Diamond suit headed by the ace. He may suspect that you hold a singleton in Diamonds.

PART II

SIGNALS AT CONTRACT BRIDGE

During the auction any bid by a player gives some information about the strength of his hand and the suit in which his strength lies.

Then during the play of the hand additional information can be exchanged by the defending partners by means of certain conventional signals. These signals are given by playing the proper card when making an opening lead, when following suit or discarding, and when trumping.

LESSON 12

SIGNALS GIVEN WHEN BIDDING

Occasionally during the bidding an opportunity arises for you or your partner to give a lead-directing signal to suggest an opening lead in a specific suit.

LEAD-DIRECTING DOUBLES

If it is obvious that you will have the opening lead, a double by your partner is considered to be a lead-directing signal in the following situations:

WHEN PARTNER DOUBLES A NO TRUMP CONTRACT

Your partner's double demands that you lead as follows:
If your partner has bid, **lead your partner's suit.**
If you have bid, but partner has not bid, **lead your own suit.**
If neither you or your partner has bid, **lead a suit which dummy bid but bid only once, and which declarer did not raise.**

If dummy has bid 2 such suits, lead the suit he bid first.

WHEN PARTNER DOUBLES A RESPONSE TO BLACKWOOD

Your partner's double suggests that you lead the suit he doubled.

When the opponent on your right bids 4 No trump, using the Blackwood Convention asking for aces, the opponent on your left (when he shows how many aces he holds) may bid 5 in the suit that your partner wants you to lead.

If your partner doubles this bid of 5 in a suit, **he asks you to lead the suit he has doubled.**

If, on the other hand, your partner does not double the suit in which your opponent responds to the Blackwood call, you may reasonably assume that your partner has no special desire to see that suit led.

In the same way a lead-directing signal may be given by doubling the response to a 5 No trump bid which asks for kings.

WHEN PARTNER DOUBLES A SLAM CONTRACT

Partner's double is a lead-directing signal. It calls for an unusual lead. For explanation see Lesson 11, Page 48.

ANSWERS

6. **Lead 7 of Hearts.** Since both you and your partner have bid, his double is not a lead-directing signal. Lead as your normally would if the contract had not been doubled. Normally you would lead the suit which is probably the longest and strongest in your hand and your partner's hand combined. If your partner has bid, usually lead your partner's suit instead of your own.

7. **Lead 8 of Hearts.** If you have made a takeout double and your partner passes, allowing the double to stand, you know that your partner has great length and strength in the trump suit. Such a penalty pass by your partner invites you to lead trumps.

8. **Lead K of Spades.** Your partner must have great length and strength in the trump suit. His penalty pass invites you to lead trumps. If, however, your hand provides a strong attacking lead, which will not risk the loss of a high card, it is better to make the attacking lead.

9. **Lead 8 of Clubs.** When your partner doubles your opponent's response to a Blackwood 4 No trump bid, his double is a "lead-directing" signal. Your partner's double suggests that you lead the suit he has doubled.

   If your partner had not doubled the 5 Club response you could reasonably assume that he had no real desire to see Clubs led.

LESSON 13

SIGNALS GIVEN WHEN MAKING AN OPENING LEAD

When your partner makes an opening lead, the card he selects gives you information about the other cards he holds in the same suit.

LEAD OF HONOR CARD

As a general rule you do not lead an honor unless you hold 2 honors in sequence.

There are, however, 2 exceptions to this general rule.

1. Against a trump contract the A is led when it is not backed by the K.
2. From a doubleton headed by an honor the higher card is led.

As a general rule when you lead one of 2 honors which are in sequence, you lead the highest honor in sequence. You lead the highest of the equal or touching honors.

There is, however, one exception to this general rule.

1. The K is led from a 3-card or longer suit headed A K.

This exception does not apply when you lead a long solid suit or a very long, almost solid suit against a No trump contract. From such a suit the A is led.

Consequently, when your partner leads an honor, you are justified in making the following deductions.

1. *When your partner leads an A against a trump contract,* **he denies that he holds the K,** unless he is leading from an A K doubleton.
2. *When your partner leads an A against a No trump contract,* **he tells you that he has a long solid or almost solid suit.** He asks you to "unblock" by throwing away your highest card each time the suit is led.
3. *When your partner leads a K,* **he guarantees that he holds either the A or the Q,** unless he is leading from a doubleton.
4. *When your partner leads a Q or J or 10,* **he denies that he holds the next higher card and guarantees that he holds the next lower card,** unless he is leading from a doubleton.

LEAD OF CARD OTHER THAN AN HONOR

When your partner makes a conventional opening lead with a card that ranks lower than the 10, you can be sure that his card is one of the following:

1. The fourth best card from a 4-card or longer suit.°
2. The lowest card from a 3-card suit headed by 1 honor or by 2 honors not in sequence.°°
3. The highest card from a worthless 3-card suit.
4. The highest card from a doubleton.
5. A singleton.°°°

You can usually identify which of the above listed cards your partner has led if you consider the bidding and study your own hand and the dummy.

WHEN YOUR PARTNER LEADS FROM A SUIT YOU HAVE BID
The card may well be any one of the cards listed above.

WHEN YOUR PARTNER LEADS FROM A SUIT HE HAS BID
The card will always be fourth best.
Exception After your partner has opened the bidding with 1 Club, and you have raised his Club suit; then if his opening lead is a Club lower than the 10, the card might be his lowest card from a 3-Card suit headed by 1 honor or by 2 honors not in sequence.

WHEN YOUR PARTNER LEADS FROM AN UNBID SUIT
The card will usually be one of the following:

1. **Fourth best** when the lead is against a No trump contract — but seldom against a trump contract.
2. **Top of a worthless 3-card suit.**
3. **Top of a doubleton** when the lead is against a trump contract — but seldom against a No trump contract.

°   The lead of a 9 is never fourth best. The lead of an 8 is seldom fourth best.
°° Your partner will seldom lead from a 3-card suit headed by 1 honor or by 2 honors not in sequence, unless you have bid that suit.
°°° Against a No trump contract your partner will never lead a singleton, unless you have bid that suit. Against a trump contract he will seldom lead a singleton in an unbid suit, unless you have bid some other suit, showing that you probably have a quick entry.

THE RULE OF 11

When your partner makes an opening lead with a card other than an honor, you can usually figure out whether or not the lead is fourth best.

Subtract the digit on the card your partner has led from the number 11. If your partner has led fourth best the difference between these 2 numbers will show how many higher° cards are held by all players except your partner.

You can actually count such higher cards in your own hand and in the dummy, and from the bidding you can decide whether the declarer holds any such higher cards.°

If these 3 hands combined (dummy's, your own, and declarer's) contain more higher cards than the difference between 11 and the digit on the card led, the lead is not fourth best.

If the lead is not fourth best, you can usually figure out (from the bidding and from studying the cards held by you and the dummy) whether the lead is from:

1. A worthless 3-card suit, or
2. A doubleton or singleton, or
3. A 3-card suit headed by 1 honor or 2 honors not in sequence.

° Cards ranking higher than the card your partner led.

INFORMATION GIVEN BY OPENING LEAD

Lead of honor card
Denies the next higher card.
Guarantees next lower card.

Lead of A against No trump
Shows long solid suit.
Tells partner to unblock.

Lead of card other than honor
Against trump contract — — doubleton, or top of 3 cards.
Against No trump contract — fourth best, or top of 3 cards.

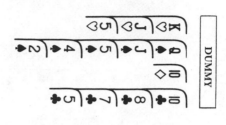

YOUR PARTNER'S HAND

DECLARER'S HAND

DUMMY

10 8 7 3	10 4 3 2	4 2	Q 9 7
♠ ♠ ♠ ♠	♡ ♡ ♡ ♡	♣ ♣	◇ ◇ ◇

YOUR OWN HAND

WHAT DOES PARTNER'S OPENING LEAD TELL YOU?

Opponents' contract is 4 Hearts.
You did not bid.
Your partner did not bid.
Partner's opening lead is Q of Clubs.

ANSWER

Your partner holds the Q J of Clubs and one or more other Clubs. He does not hold the A or K of Clubs.

Your partner's suit is not headed by either A K or K Q. If it were, in either case, he would lead the K.

Your partner's suit is not headed A Q without the J. If it were, he would lead the A from a 4-card or longer suit against a trump contract.

Your partner is not leading from a doubleton. He would almost never lead a doubleton headed by the Q, unless you had bid the suit.

The Q is certainly not a singleton. He would seldom lead a singleton, unless you had bid a suit, indicating that you have a quick entry.

Therefore, your partner's lead of the Q assures you that he holds the next lower card.

YOUR PARTNER'S HAND

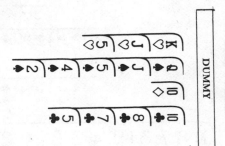

YOUR OWN HAND

WHAT DOES PARTNER'S OPENING LEAD TELL YOU?

1. Opponents' contract is 4 Hearts.
   You did not bid.
   Your partner did not bid.
   Partner's opening lead is K of Diamonds.

2. Opponents' contract is 3 No trump.
   You did not bid.
   Your partner did not bid.
   Partner's opening lead is A of Diamonds.

3. Opponents' contract is 4 Hearts.
   You did not bid.
   Your partner did not bid.
   Partner's opening lead is A of Diamonds.

ANSWERS

1. **Your partner holds the A of Diamonds.**

   The K may be led from a suit headed A K or from a suit headed K Q. Since you hold the Q of Diamonds your partner must hold the A.

2. **Your partner holds a long powerful Diamond suit which is almost solid.**

   Whenever your partner leads an A against a No trump contract he holds such a suit. He asks you to "unblock" by throwing your highest card each time the suit is led. Play your Q on the first trick and your 9 on the second trick.

3. **Your partner does not hold the K of Diamonds. He holds 3 or more Diamonds headed by the A.**

   Your partner's Diamonds are not headed by A K. If they were the K would be led against a trump contract, unless the suit is a doubleton A K. You can be almost certain that your partner does not have a doubleton A K. Your partner would avoid leading a doubleton A K because he can not count on you for a quick entry, since you did not bid a suit.

   The conclusion that your partner holds 3 or more Diamonds **is based on the following considerations.**

   You can be almost certain that he is not leading from a doubleton A x. If he were, the declarer would hold 7 Diamonds. This is very unlikely.

   Therefore, you can reasonably assume that your partner does not hold the K and that he does hold at least 3 Diamonds.

YOUR PARTNER'S HAND

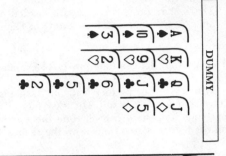

DECLARER'S HAND

DUMMY

| 9 7 4 | J 10 6 | K 10 8 7 4 | A 2 |
| ♠ ♠ ♠ | ♡ ♡ ♡ | ♣ ♣ ♣ ♣ ♣ | ◇ ◇ |

YOUR OWN HAND

WHAT DOES PARTNER'S OPENING LEAD TELL YOU?

1.

Opponents' contract is 3 No trump.
You did not bid.
Your partner did not bid.
Partner's opening lead is 7 of Hearts.

2.

Opponents' contract is 4 Spades.
You did not bid.
Your partner did not bid.
Partner's opening lead is 3 of Hearts.

ANSWERS

1. **Your partner is leading his highest card from a worthless 3-
card suit.**

   You can reasonably assume that your partner's lead is not
   fourth best. By subtracting 7 from 11 you know that there
   would be only 4 cards higher than the 7 outside your partner's
   hand, if your partner's lead were fourth best. In your hand
   and the dummy you can count 4 such cards. Declarer probably

holds at least 1 honor in Hearts, because he bid No trump. So apparently there are at least 5 cards higher than the 7 outside of your partner's hand.

Your partner is probably not leading low from a suit headed 1 honor or 2 honors not in sequence, nor is he leading from a doubleton or singleton. Against a No trump contract he would almost never lead from any such suits, unless you had bid that suit.

Your partner must be leading the top of a 3-card suit.

2. **Your partner is leading fourth best from a worthless 4-card suit. Declarer holds 3 Hearts headed A Q.**

By applying the Rule of 11 you can see that your partner's lead is probably fourth best. By subtracting 3 from 11 you know that there are 8 cards higher than the 3 outside your partner's hand. In your hand and the dummy you can count only 5 of these cards. Declarer may well hold 3 Hearts higher than the 3 spot.

The conclusion that your partner is leading fourth best is confirmed by further evidence.

Your partner is not leading his highest card from a worthless 3-card suit, or a doubleton. The only Heart lower than the 3 is showing in the dummy.

Your partner is not leading a singleton. It is hardly possible that the declarer holds 6 Hearts when the contract is 4 Spades.

Your partner is probably not leading low from a 3-card suit headed by 1 honor or 2 honors not in sequence. He would avoid leading such a suit, unless you had bid it.

The conclusion that your partner's suit is a worthless 4-card suit is based on the following considerations.

The only honor cards in the Heart suit that you can not see in your own hand and in the dummy are the A and Q.

Your partner does not hold the A. From a 4-card suit headed by the A he would lead the A against a trump contract.

Your partner does not hold the Q. He would avoid leading from a 4-card suit headed by only 1 honor unless you had bid the suit.

Therefore you are reasonably certain that your partner is leading from a worthless 4-card suit.

YOUR PARTNER'S HAND

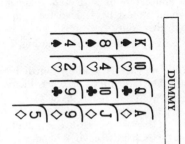

DECLARER'S HAND

DUMMY

YOUR OWN HAND

WHAT DOES PARTNER'S OPENING LEAD TELL YOU?

1. Opponents' contract is 2 Spades.
   You opened the bidding with 1 Heart.
   Your partner raised your Hearts.
   Partner's opening lead is 7 of Hearts.

2. Opponents' contract is 2 Spades.
   You bid 1 Heart.
   Your partner did not raise your Hearts.
   Partner's opening lead is 3 of Hearts.

ANSWERS

1. **Your partner is leading low from a 3-card suit — K 8 7.**

   Your partner is not leading fourth best. When you subtract 7 from 11 you get 4. If your partner's lead were fourth best there would be only 4 cards higher than the 7 outside your partner's hand. You can count 4 higher cards in your own hand and the dummy.

   If your partner held both the A and K, he would have led the K. If he held the A without the K, he would have led the A. So the A must be in declarer's hand. Therefore you know that there are at least 5 cards higher than the 7 outside your partner's hand and that your partner is not leading fourth best.

   Your partner is not leading from a worthless 3-card suit, a doubleton, or a singleton. Your partner raised your Hearts, so you know he has adequate trump support. Three small trumps are not adequate support. He must hold an honor in Hearts.

   Therefore, you know that your partner is leading low from a 3-card suit — K 8 7.

2. **Your partner is probably leading a singleton.**

   Your partner's lead can not be the top of a 3-card suit or a doubleton. The only Heart lower than the 3 is in dummy's hand.

   Your partner probably is not leading fourth best, nor is he leading low from a 3-card suit headed by the A or K. He did not raise your Hearts, even though your opponents did not bid beyond 2 Spades. Your partner probably lacks adequate trump support for your Hearts. In that case he can not have 4 Hearts or 3 Hearts headed by the A or K.

LESSON 14

SIGNALS GIVEN WHEN FOLLOWING SUIT
OR DISCARDING

You give your partner important information about your hand by the card you play when you follow suit or discard.

WHEN YOU TRY TO TAKE THE TRICK

When you are trying to win the trick, you play the lowest card you hold which will serve your purpose.

If you hold high cards in sequence, you play the lowest card in the sequence.

If at the top of your suit you hold a tenace over the highest card exposed in the dummy, and that high card is not played from the dummy, you play the lower card of your tenace.

Therefore, when you play a card with which obviously you are trying to take the trick, you tell your partner that you do not have a lower card in sequence, or a lower card which will serve the same purpose.

WHEN YOU DO NOT TRY TO TAKE THE TRICK

The first time your partner leads a suit, and you are not trying to win the trick, you can give your partner important information by the card you play.

You can give him either an encouraging "come-on" signal, suggesting that he should lead that suit again; or you can give him a discouraging "warning" signal, suggesting that he should avoid that suit.

Likewise, when you discard because you can not follow suit, you can give your partner either a "come-on" signal, asking him to lead the suit from which you discard; or you can give him a "warning" signal, asking him not to lead that suit.

You give your partner a discouraging signal **when you play your lowest card in a suit.** This discouraging signal is further emphasized if later you play a higher card in the same suit.

You give your partner an encouraging signal **when you play an unnecessarily high card (not your lowest) in a suit.** This encouraging signal is further emphasized if later you play a lower card in the same suit. This high-low play is called an "echo."

Whenever you play high to give an encouraging "come-on" signal, make your signal as clear as possible by playing the highest card you can afford to part with. Do not hesitate to signal with an honor, unless this honor must be saved to take a trick.

A necessary guard to a possible trick winning card in the suit you want your partner to lead should not be discarded in order to signal your partner to lead that suit.

Therefore, if you can not spare a discard in the suit you want your partner to lead, your only means of calling for a lead in that suit is to discard your lowest cards in other suits. This invites a lead in the suit you want by the process of elimination.

WHEN DUMMY HOLDS LONG SUIT BUT NO ENTRIES

When dummy holds a long strong suit, but no entries in other suits, your partner may hold a stopper in that suit. If so, he does not want to play his stopper so long as declarer can still lead dummy's long suit.

When dummy's suit is led, or when you discard from dummy's suit, you can let your partner know how many cards you hold in that suit. Then he will know when to play his stopper.

If you play your lowest card first and later follow with a higher card you tell your partner that you hold exactly 3 cards in that suit.

If, however, you play first high then low you tell your partner that you do not hold exactly 3 cards. In this case your partner can almost always tell whether you hold 2 cards or 4 cards in that suit.

WHEN FOLLOWING SUIT OR DISCARDING

When you are trying to win a trick
Play of any card denies a lower card serving same purpose.

To encourage lead of suit
Play high, or first high then low.

To discourage lead of suit
Play low, or first low then high.

When dummy holds a long strong suit, but no entries in other suits
If you hold exactly 3 cards —— Play first low, then high in that suit.
If you hold 2 cards or 4 cards — Play first high, then low in that suit.

YOUR PARTNER'S HAND

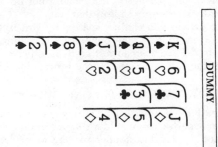

YOUR OWN HAND

WHAT SIGNAL DO YOU GIVE YOUR PARTNER?

1. Opponents' contact is 3 No trump.
   When declarer runs his Spade suit, how can you signal your
   partner to lead Hearts?

2. Opponents' contract is 3 No trump.
   Partner's opening lead is 8 of Diamonds.
   Dummy plays 4 of Diamonds.
   What card do you play?

3. Opponents' contract is 3 No trump.
   When Spades are led, what card will you play?

ANSWERS

1. **After your Spades are exhausted, signal for a lead of Hearts by discarding first your lowest Club and then your lowest Diamond.**

   These discards will warn your partner not to lead Clubs and Diamonds. By the process of elimination you invite a lead of Hearts. Do not signal your partner to lead Hearts by discarding the 8 of Hearts, because you must keep the 8 to guard the K and Q.

2. **Play the 10 of Diamonds.** When you play the 10 you tell your partner that you do not hold the 9 of Diamonds, because you have played the lowest card in your hand which will serve your purpose.

   When you play the 10, you do not deny that you hold the Q, because with J in the dummy the 10 serves the same purpose as the Q.

3. **Play the 5 of Spades first and the 7 of Spades next.** Dummy holds a long, strong Spade suit, but no entries in other suits. If your partner holds the A and 2 small Spades, he does not want to play the A so long as the declarer can still lead Spades.

   When you play your lowest card first and later follow with a higher card, you tell your partner that you hold exactly 3 cards in that suit. Then he knows that he can safely play the A on the second round of Spades.

| YOUR PARTNER'S HAND |

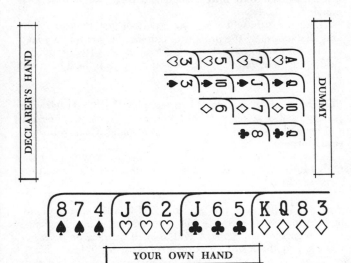

| YOUR OWN HAND |

WHAT SIGNAL DO YOU GIVE YOUR PARTNER?

1. Opponents' contract is 4 Hearts.
   Partner's opening lead is A of Diamonds.
   What card do you play?

2. Opponents' contract is 4 Hearts.
   Partner's opening lead is K of Spades.
   What card do you play?

3. Opponents' contract is 3 No trump.
   Partner's opening lead is 9 of Diamonds.
   What card do you play?

ANSWERS

1. **Play the 8 of Diamonds.** When you follow suit with a higher card than necessary, you give your partner a "come-on" signal, suggesting that he should lead the suit again.

2. **Play the 4 of Spades.** When you follow suit with your lowest card, you give your partner a discouraging signal, warning him not to lead that suit again.

3. **Play the Q of Diamonds.** When you are trying to win the trick, play the lowest card that will serve your purpose. If you hold 2 high cards in sequence, play the lower card of the sequence.

WHAT CARD WILL YOU PLAY?

1.

| 9 7 3 | A 10 9 6 4 | Q J 10 7 3 |
| ♠ ♠ ♠ | ♦ ♦ ♦ ♦ ♦ | ♣ ♣ ♣ ♣ ♣ |

Opponents' contract is 4 Spades.
Your partner did not bid.
When trumps are led, what card will you play?

2.

| Q 9 2 | K J 10 4 3 2 | A 10 9 4 |
| ♠ ♠ ♠ | ♦ ♦ ♦ ♦ ♦ ♦ | ♣ ♣ ♣ ♣ |

Opponents' contract is 4 Spades.
Your partner did not bid.
When trumps are led, what card will you play?

3.

| 9 3 | Q 10 9 7 5 2 | A 10 9 7 6 |
| ♠ ♠ | ♦ ♦ ♦ ♦ ♦ ♦ | ♣ ♣ ♣ ♣ ♣ |

Opponents' contract is 4 Spades.
Your partner bid Hearts.
Partner's opening lead is 4 of Hearts.
When you ruff this trick, what card will you play?

4.

| 9 6 4 | Q 10 9 7 5 | A 10 9 7 6 |
| ♠ ♠ ♠ | ♦ ♦ ♦ ♦ ♦ | ♣ ♣ ♣ ♣ ♣ |

Opponents' contract is 4 Spades.
Your partner bid Hearts.
Partner's opening lead is 4 of Hearts.
When you ruff this trick, what card will you play?

ANSWERS

1. **Play 7 of Spades.** You hold 3 trumps and there is a suit you want to ruff. When trumps are led, you can give your partner this information by following suit first with your middle trump and next with your lowest trump.

2. **Play 2 of Spades.** You hold 3 trumps and there is a suit which you can ruff. However, you do not want to ruff. You can not spare a trump for that purpose. You need all your low trumps to guard the Q.

3. **Play 3 of Spades.** If you hold only 2 trumps, ruff with your lowest trump. If you ruff with the 3 first and later with the 9 your partner will know that you can not ruff a third time.

4. **Play 6 of Spades.** You hold 3 trumps. If you ruff first high then low, you tell your partner you still have a trump left with which you can ruff a third time, if the suit is led again.

LESSON 16

SUIT-PREFERENCE SIGNAL

The suit-preference signal is a convention used by experienced players. It is a signal used to call for the lead of a specific suit, before you have a chance to do so by means of a high discard in the desired suit, or by means of low discards in other suits.

A suit-preference signal can be given either when you lead, or when you follow suit.

WHEN YOU LEAD

Sometimes you lead when it is obvious that your partner will trump the trick, and that there are only two other suits through which he might hope to throw the lead back into your hand. In this case you can indicate to him which of these two suits to lead back, so you can recapture the lead and give him an opportunity to trump again.

If you lead an unnecessarily high card you tell your partner to lead back the higher ranking of the two suits.

If you lead your lowest card you tell him to lead back the lower ranking suit.

WHEN YOU FOLLOW SUIT

Sometimes your partner leads a sure winner, and the cards in the dummy show beyond any shadow of a doubt that your partner should not continue to lead this same suit. In this case, if there are only 2 other suits to which he might advantageously shift, you can indicate to him which of these 2 suits you prefer.

If you follow suit with an unnecessarily high card you tell him to shift to the higher ranking of the two suits.

If you follow suit with your lowest card you tell him to shift to the lower ranking suit.

A suit-preference signal must not be given, unless it is perfectly obvious that the suit in which a lead is desired can only be one of 2 suits.

A suit-preference signal must not be attempted if there is any possibility that it might be mistaken for a conventional high, encouraging, "come-on" signal; or for a low, discouraging, warning signal.

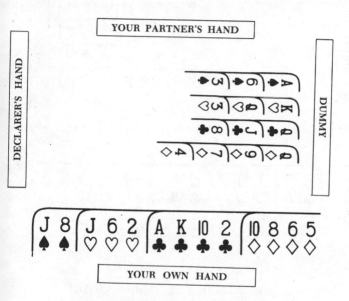

SUIT-PREFERENCE SIGNAL

When signal can not be mistaken.
When obviously partner must select lead from one of two suits only.
Play unnecessarily high card to suggest lead of higher ranking suit.
Play lowest card . . . . to suggest lead of lower ranking suit.

HOW DO YOU SIGNAL FOR THE LEAD YOU WANT?

Opponents' contract is 4 Spades.
Partner's opening lead is A of Hearts.
What card do you play?

ANSWER

Play 2 of Hearts. Your partner will recognize that it is unnecessary for you to give him a conventional warning signal asking him not to continue leading Hearts. Therefore, your low card must be a suit-preference signal asking him to lead Clubs, which is the lower ranking of the 2 suits other than trumps.

YOUR PARTNER'S HAND

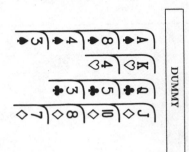

YOUR OWN HAND

HOW DO YOU SIGNAL FOR THE LEAD YOU WANT?
Opponents' contract is 4 Spades.
Partner's opening lead is A of Hearts.
What card do you play?

ANSWER
Play J of Hearts. It is so obvious that your partner should not
lead another Heart that he will not mistake your high card for
a conventional "come-on" signal asking him to continue leading
Hearts. There are only 2 other suits which you might want him
to lead — Diamonds and Clubs. If you play a high card on the
first trick, you tell him to lead the higher ranking of these 2
suits, which is Diamonds.

YOUR PARTNER'S HAND

DUMMY

DECLARER'S HAND

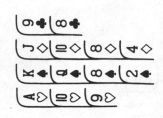

YOUR OWN HAND

HOW DO YOU SIGNAL FOR THE LEAD YOU WANT?

Opponents' contract is 4 Hearts.
You opened leading A of Spades.
Your partner did not follow suit.
What card do you lead next?

ANSWER

Lead J of Spades. Your partner will trump your second lead of Spades. If he knows which suit to lead back to get into your hand again, he can probably trump a second Spade. There are obviously only 2 suits through which he can hope to put you back in the lead — Diamonds and Clubs. If you now lead the J of Spades, which is a high card, you tell him to lead back the higher ranking of the 2 suits, which is Diamonds.

YOUR PARTNER'S HAND

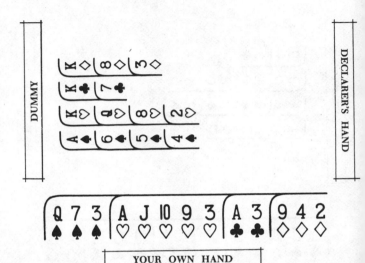

DUMMY

DECLARER'S HAND

| Q 7 3 | A J 10 9 3 | A 3 | 9 4 2 |
| ♠ ♠ ♠ | ♡ ♡ ♡ ♡ ♡ | ♣ ♣ | ♢ ♢ ♢ |

YOUR OWN HAND

HOW DO YOU SIGNAL FOR THE LEAD YOU WANT?

Opponents' Contract is 4 Spades.
You opened leading A of Hearts.
Your partner did not follow suit.
What card do you lead next?

ANSWER

Lead 3 of Hearts. When your partner gets the lead by trumping the second round of Hearts you want him to lead a Club. This is the only way you can get the lead again and return another Heart for him to trump. If you now lead the 3 of Hearts, which is a low card, you tell him to lead back the lower ranking of the 2 suits — Diamonds and Clubs.

PART III

QUIZZES

QUIZ 1

1. WHAT IS YOUR OPENING LEAD?

Your opponents' contract is 1 No trump.
No suit was bid by your partner or your opponents.
You are West. The bidding was as follows:

SOUTH	WEST	NORTH	EAST
1 No trump	Pass	Pass	Pass

2. WHAT IS YOUR OPENING LEAD?

Your opponents' contract is 2 No trump.
Your partner bid Diamonds.
No suit was bid by either of your opponents.
You are West. The bidding was as follows:

SOUTH	WEST	NORTH	EAST
1 No trump	Pass	Pass	2 Diamonds
2 No trump	Pass	Pass	Pass

3. WHAT IS YOUR OPENING LEAD?

Your opponents' contract is 4 Spades.
Your partner did not bid.
You are West. The bidding was as follows:

SOUTH	WEST	NORTH	EAST
1 Spade	2 Clubs	2 Diamonds	Pass
3 Spades	Pass	4 Spades	Pass
Pass	Pass		

4. WHAT IS YOUR OPENING LEAD?

Your opponents' contract is 5 Diamonds.
Your partner bid Hearts.
You are West. The bidding was as follows:

SOUTH	WEST	NORTH	EAST
1 Diamond	2 Clubs	2 Spades	3 Hearts
4 Diamonds	4 Hearts	5 Diamonds	Double
Pass	Pass	Pass	

ANSWERS

1. LEAD 4 OF CLUBS
The suit to lead is Clubs.
When your partner has not bid, as a general rule lead your own longest and strongest suit against a No trump contract.
The card to lead is the 4.
Against a No trump contract, when you lead a suit which was not bid by your partner, always lead fourth best unless your suit is headed by a leadable sequence.

2. LEAD 7 OF DIAMONDS
The suit to lead is Diamonds.
Your partner's Diamond suit may not turn out to be any stronger than your own Club suit. But against a No trump contract, whenever you are in doubt whether your partner's suit or your own suit is the longest and strongest suit in the combined hands, lead your partner's suit.
The card to lead is the 7.
When you lead from a worthless 3-card suit, always lead the highest card.°

3. LEAD K OF CLUBS
The suit to lead is Clubs.
A lead from a 4-card or longer suit headed A K is a very good attacking lead.
The card to lead is the K.
Against a trump contract, when you lead from a 4-card or longer suit headed by 2 honors in sequence, lead an honor instead of fourth best.

4. LEAD K OF CLUBS
The suit to lead is Clubs.
Here you have a choice between 2 good attacking leads, your Clubs and your partner's Hearts. The first lead of Hearts might well be trumped, because your partner probably has at least 5 Hearts and you have 4.
Lead your K of Clubs and take a look at dummy. Then switch to Hearts, if it appears advisable.

°Unless you agreed with your partner, before the game started, to lead the lowest card, as some experts do.

QUIZ 2

1. WHAT IS YOUR OPENING LEAD?
Your opponents' contract is 3 No trump.
No suit was bid by your partner or by your opponents.
You are West. The bidding was as follows:

SOUTH	WEST	NORTH	EAST
1 No trump	Pass	2 No trump	Pass
3 No trump	Pass	Pass	Pass

2. WHAT IS YOUR OPENING LEAD?
Your opponents' contract is 3 No trump.
Your partner bid Diamonds.
No suit was bid by either of your opponents.
You are West. The bidding was as follows:

EAST	SOUTH	WEST	NORTH
1 Diamond	1 No trump	Pass	2 No trump
Pass	3 No trump	Pass	Pass
Pass			

3. WHAT IS YOUR OPENING LEAD?
Your opponents' contract is 3 No trump.
Your partner did not bid.
Your left hand opponent bid Spades.
You are West. The bidding was as follows:

SOUTH	WEST	NORTH	EAST
1 Club	Pass	1 Spade	Pass
2 No trump	Pass	3 No trump	Pass
Pass	Pass		

4. WHAT IS YOUR OPENING LEAD?
Your opponents' contract is 4 Hearts.
Your partner did not bid.
You are West. The bidding was as follows:

SOUTH	WEST	NORTH	EAST
1 Heart	Pass	2 Diamonds	Pass
3 Hearts	Pass	4 Hearts	Pass
Pass	Pass		

ANSWERS

1. **LEAD 4 OF SPADES**
   The suit to lead is Spades.
   Since your partner did not bid, lead your own longest suit.
   The card to lead is the 4.
   When you lead from a 4-card or longer suit which does not contain any honors, always lead fourth best.

2. **LEAD Q OF DIAMONDS**
   The suit to lead is Diamonds.
   You have strong support for your partner's Diamond suit. It is certainly the strongest suit in the combined hands.
   The card to lead is the Q.
   From a 3-card suit headed by 2 touching honors, other than the A K, always lead the highest card in the suit.

3. **LEAD Q OF DIAMONDS**
   The suit to lead is Diamonds.
   If your only long suit was bid by your opponents, and it is not headed by a solid sequence, make a protecting short suit lead, instead of leading from your own longest suit. Against a No trump contract prefer a 3-card suit to a doubleton, unless the 3-card suit is headed by 1 honor or 2 honors not in sequence.
   A lead from Q J x is not a desirable protecting lead, but it is acceptable if no better lead is available.
   The card to lead is the Q.
   When you lead from a 3-card suit headed by K Q, Q J, or J 10, always lead the higher of the 2 honors.

4. **LEAD 9 OF CLUBS**
   The suit to lead is Clubs.
   When no good attacking or ruffing lead is available, make a protecting lead.
   Not only is a doubleton a safe lead against a trump contract, but also it offers a bare possibility that you may be able to trump the third round of Clubs with your 7 of Hearts.
   The card to lead is the 9.
   From any doubleton lead the highest card.

1. WHAT IS YOUR OPENING LEAD?

Your opponents' contract is 3 No trump.
No suit was bid by your partner or your opponents.
You are West. The bidding was as follows:

SOUTH	WEST	NORTH	EAST
1 No trump	Pass	2 No trump	Pass
3 No trump	Pass	Pass	Pass

2. WHAT IS YOUR OPENING LEAD?

Your opponents' contract is 3 No trump.
Your partner bid Diamonds.
You are West. The bidding was as follows:

SOUTH	WEST	NORTH	EAST
1 Club	Pass	1 Spade	2 Diamonds
2 No trump	3 Diamonds	Pass	Pass
3 No trump	Pass	Pass	Pass

3. WHAT IS YOUR OPENING LEAD?

Your opponents' contract is 3 Spades.
Your partner bid Diamonds.
You are West. The bidding was as follows:

SOUTH	WEST	NORTH	EAST
1 Spade	Pass	Pass	2 Diamonds
2 Hearts	Pass	2 Spades	Pass
3 Spades	Pass	Pass	Pass

ANSWERS

1. **LEAD 4 OF HEARTS**
   The suit to lead is Hearts.

   Your Heart suit is stronger than your Diamond suit, but it does not provide a good attacking lead. Nevertheless, lead Hearts, since you have no good protecting lead.

   You can not afford to lead Clubs. You will need your A and K of Clubs for entries. Do not lead Spades. The lead of a doubleton is not a very good protecting lead against No trump.

   The card to lead is the 4.

   When you lead from a 4-card or longer suit, as a general rule, lead fourth best.

2. **LEAD 2 OF DIAMONDS**
   The suit to lead is Diamonds.

   Since your partner bid Diamonds, and you have strong support for his suit, Diamonds is obviously the suit to lead, because it is the strongest in your hand and your partner's hand combined.

   The card to lead is the 2.

   Against a No trump contract, when you lead from 4 cards or more in your partner's suit, lead fourth best unless you hold 2 honors in sequence, or a leadable sequence.

3. **LEAD 10 OF SPADES**
   The suit to lead is Spades.

   Here a trump lead is obviously indicated. You have reason to suspect that dummy is short in the Heart suit. He denied Heart support when he preferred declarer's Spades.

   Don't give declarer a chance to get rid of losing Hearts by trumping them in the dummy. Shorten dummy's trump holding by leading trumps.

   Do not lead your partner's Diamonds, even though it is a good attacking lead. A trump lead in this case is much better.

   The card to lead is the 10.

   Lead the highest card from a doubleton.

QUIZ 3 (continued)

4. WHAT IS YOUR OPENING LEAD?
Your opponents' contract is 4 Spades.
Your partner did not bid.
You are West. The bidding was as follows:

SOUTH	WEST	NORTH	EAST
1 Spade	Pass	2 Spades	Pass
4 Spades	Pass	Pass	Pass

5. WHAT IS YOUR OPENING LEAD?
Your opponents' contract is 3 No trump.
Your partner doubled.
No suit was bid by either you or your partner.
Dummy bid Spades and Hearts.
You are West. The bidding was as follows:

SOUTH	WEST	NORTH	EAST
1 Diamond	Pass	1 Spade	Pass
2 No trump	Pass	3 Hearts	Pass
3 No trump	Pass	Pass	Double
Pass	Pass	Pass	

6. WHAT IS YOUR OPENING LEAD?
Your opponents' contract is 3 No trump.
No suit was bid by you or your partner.
You are West. The bidding was as follows:

SOUTH	WEST	NORTH	EAST
1 Diamond	Pass	1 Spade	Pass
2 Hearts	Pass	3 Hearts	Pass
3 No trump	Pass	Pass	Pass

ANSWERS

4. LEAD 10 OF SPADES
The suit to lead is Spades.

Against a trump contract, when no good attacking or ruffing lead is available, make a protecting lead. A trump lead is an acceptable protecting lead when you have 2 or 3 small trumps.

But even if you had a good attacking lead, a trump lead would be preferred in this situation. The bidding indicates that declarer has a strong hand, and that dummy has a minimum responding hand. Part of dummy's strength may well be a short suit. A trump lead will help exhaust dummy's trumps before declarer can use them for ruffing.

The card to lead is the 10.

From a doubleton, always lead the highest card.

5. LEAD 10 OF SPADES
The suit to lead is Spades.

When your partner doubles a No trump contract, if neither you nor your partner has bid a suit, lead a suit which was bid by the dummy, provided it was not rebid by the dummy or raised by the declarer. If dummy has bid 2 suits, lead the suit he bid first.

The card to lead is the 10.

Always lead the top card from a doubleton.

6. LEAD K OF CLUBS
The suit to lead is Clubs.

You have no good attacking lead. Do not lead Spades, Hearts, or Diamonds. Avoid any suit bid by your opponents, unless you hold a solid sequence.

A lead from a 3-card suit headed by 2 honors in sequence is not a desirable protecting lead, but it is acceptable when no better lead is available.

The card to lead is the K.

From a 3-card suit headed A K, always lead the K.

QUIZ 4

1. **WHAT IS YOUR OPENING LEAD?**
   Your opponents' contract is 3 No trump.
   No suit was bid by your partner or by your opponents.
   You are West. The bidding was as follows:

SOUTH	WEST	NORTH	EAST
1 No trump	Pass	3 No trump	Pass
Pass	Pass		

2. **WHAT IS YOUR OPENING LEAD?**
   Your opponents' contract is 3 No trump.
   Your partner bid Hearts.
   You are West. The bidding was as follows:

NORTH	EAST	SOUTH	WEST
1 Club	1 Heart	1 No trump	Pass
2 No trump	Pass	3 No trump	Pass
Pass	Pass		

3. **WHAT IS YOUR OPENING LEAD?**
   Your opponents' contract is 4 Spades.
   Your partner bid Clubs.
   You are West. The bidding was as follows:

EAST	SOUTH	WEST	NORTH
1 Club	1 Spade	Pass	2 Spades
3 Clubs	3 Spades	4 Clubs	4 Spades
Pass	Pass	Pass	

ANSWERS

1. LEAD 3 OF DIAMONDS
The suit to lead is Diamonds.
Since your partner did not bid, lead your own longest and strongest suit. Against a No trump contract do not hesitate to lead from a 5-card suit, even though it is headed by a high tenace.
The card to lead is the 3.
Against a No trump contract, when you lead from a 4-card or longer suit which was not bid by your partner, lead fourth best, unless your suit is headed by a leadable sequence.

2. LEAD 2 OF HEARTS
The suit to lead is Hearts.
Your Diamond suit is not a very strong suit, because it is headed by a tenace. Therefore, lead your partner's suit in preference to your own, even though you have only a singleton in your partner's suit. The fact that declarer bid No trump over your partner's Heart bid should not make you afraid to lead your partner's suit.

3. LEAD 2 OF CLUBS
The suit to lead is Clubs.
Against a trump contract a lead from your partner's suit is a good attacking lead.
Do not lead your singleton Heart. You hold 3 "extra" trumps, but you do not have a stopper in trumps. Declarer will draw your Spades before you get a chance to trump.
The card to lead is the 2.
When you lead your partner's suit against a trump contract, lead fourth best, unless you hold the A, or 2 honors in sequence, or a leadable sequence.

QUIZ 4 (continued)

4. WHAT IS YOUR OPENING LEAD?
Your opponents' contract is 3 Clubs.
Your partner did not bid.
You are West. The bidding was as follows:

SOUTH	WEST	NORTH	EAST
1 Club	Pass	1 Spade	Pass
3 Clubs	Pass	Pass	Pass

5. WHAT IS YOUR OPENING LEAD?
Your opponents' contract is 4 Spades.
Your partner bid Hearts.
You are West. The bidding was as follows:

NORTH	EAST	SOUTH	WEST
1 Club	1 Heart	1 Spade	Pass
3 Spades	Pass	4 Spades	Pass
Pass	Pass		

6. WHAT IS YOUR OPENING LEAD?
Your opponents' contract is 4 Spades.
Your partner did not bid.
You are West. The bidding was as follows:

NORTH	EAST	SOUTH	WEST
1 Club	Pass	1 Spade	Pass
3 Spades	Pass	4 Spades	Pass
Pass	Pass		

ANSWERS

4. LEAD A OF DIAMONDS
The suit to lead is Diamonds.

Against a trump contract, if you have 4 or more trumps, lead the suit you would open against a No trump contract. Lead from your 5-card Diamond suit, even though it is headed by a high tenace.

Try to establish your Diamond suit and make the declarer exhaust his trumps by ruffing your Diamonds. The fact that your opponents did not end up with a No trump contract indicates that they may not be able to take more than 1 Diamond trick. The fact that they did not arrive at a game contract indicates that your partner may have some high card strength. If so he will probably be able to secure the lead and return your Diamond suit more than once.

The card to lead is the A.

When you lead from a 4-card or longer suit headed by the A against a trump contract, lead the A instead of fourth best.

5. LEAD 2 OF HEARTS
The suit to lead is Hearts.

When you have "extra" trumps, a singleton in your partner's suit is an excellent ruffing lead, even if you do not hold a stopper in the trump suit.

Since your partner has bid Hearts, you have reason to hope that he can take the first trick and will lead back a losing Heart for you to trump, before declarer can draw your trumps.

6. LEAD 3 OF SPADES
The suit to lead is Spades.

The Diamond suit does not provide a good attacking lead. If you lead out the A of Diamonds you will probably take only 1 Diamond trick. Wait until Diamonds are led up to you.

The singleton Heart is not a good ruffing lead. You have no reason to think that your partner can get the lead and return the Heart suit before declarer has taken out your trumps.

For a protecting lead you must choose between trumps or Clubs. Prefer the trump lead, because dummy bid Clubs.

The card to lead is the 3.

From a 3-card suit headed by a single honor other than the A, always lead low.

QUIZ 5

1. WHAT IS YOUR OPENING LEAD?
Your opponents' contract is 3 No trump.
No suit was bid by your partner or by your opponents.
You are West. The bidding was as follows:

SOUTH	WEST	NORTH	EAST
1 No trump	Pass	2 No trump	Pass
3 No trump	Pass	Pass	Pass

2. WHAT IS YOUR OPENING LEAD?
Your opponents' contract is 3 No trump.
Your partner bid Clubs.
You are West. The bidding was as follows:

NORTH	EAST	SOUTH	WEST
1 Heart	2 Clubs	2 No trump	3 Clubs
3 No trump	Pass	Pass	Pass

3. WHAT IS YOUR OPENING LEAD?
Your opponents' contract is 3 No trump.
Dummy bid Diamonds.
Your partner did not bid.
You are West. The bidding was as follows:

NORTH	EAST	SOUTH	WEST
1 Diamond	Pass	1 No trump	Pass
3 No trump	Pass	Pass	Pass

ANSWERS

1. LEAD K OF DIAMONDS
The suit to lead is Diamonds.
Your Diamonds are stronger than your Spades. A 4-card suit headed by an interrupted sequence provides a strong attacking lead. Do not lead Spades. Avoid leading from a 4-card suit headed by only 1 honor.
The card to lead is the K.
When you lead from a 4-card or longer suit headed by a leadable sequence, lead an honor instead of fourth best. When you lead from an interrupted sequence not headed A K, always lead the highest honor.

2. LEAD 9 OF CLUBS
The suit to lead is Clubs.
Against a No trump contract, as a general rule, lead the suit which is probably the longest and strongest suit in your hand and your partner's hand combined. If your partner has bid, usually lead your partner's suit instead of your own.
   Do not hesitate to lead your partner's suit, even though declarer bid No trump over your partner's bid of 2 Clubs.
The card to lead is the 9.
When you lead from a 3-card suit which contains no honors, always lead the highest card.°

3. LEAD 9 OF CLUBS
The suit to lead is Clubs.
Your Diamond suit is your strongest suit, but do not lead it, because it was bid by your opponents, and it is not headed by a solid sequence. Do not lead Spades. Avoid a 4-card suit headed by a single honor. Make a protecting short suit lead. A worthless 3-card suit offers a good protecting lead.
The card to lead is the 9.
Always lead the highest card from a worthless 3-card suit.°

° Unless, before the game started, you agreed with your partner to lead the lowest card from a worthless 3-card suit, as some experts do.

QUIZ 5 (continued)

4. **WHAT IS YOUR OPENING LEAD?**
   Your opponents' contract is 4 Hearts.
   Your partner bid Clubs.
   You are West. The bidding was as follows:

NORTH	EAST	SOUTH	WEST
1 Spade	2 Clubs	2 Hearts	3 Clubs
4 Hearts	Pass	Pass	Pass

5. **WHAT IS YOUR OPENING LEAD?**
   Your opponents' contract is 3 Clubs.
   Your partner did not bid.
   You are West. The bidding was as follows:

NORTH	EAST	SOUTH	WEST
1 Diamond	Pass	2 Clubs	Pass
2 Diamonds	Pass	3 Clubs	Pass
Pass	Pass		

6. **WHAT IS YOUR OPENING LEAD?**
   Your opponents' contract is 3 No trump.
   Your partner did not bid.
   You are West. The bidding was as follows:

NORTH	EAST	SOUTH	WEST
1 Diamond	Pass	2 Clubs	Pass
2 Hearts	Pass	2 No trump	Pass
3 No trump	Pass	Pass	Pass

4. LEAD K OF DIAMONDS
The suit to lead is Diamonds.
Here you have a choice between 2 good attacking leads —
your partner's Clubs or your own Diamonds. A lead from a
4-card or longer suit headed by an interrupted sequence is
always a good attacking lead. Against a trump contract it is
probably better to lead from such a suit than to lead your partner's suit.
The card to lead is the K.
Whenever you lead from a suit headed by a leadable sequence,
lead an honor instead of fourth best. When you lead from an
interrupted sequence, always lead the highest honor unless
the 2 top honors are A K.

5. LEAD 8 OF HEARTS
The suit to lead is Hearts.
The Diamond suit is not a good attacking lead. Avoid any
suit bid by an opponent unless your cards in that suit are
headed by a solid sequence. The Spade suit should not be
led because it is headed by a single honor.
The low Heart doubleton provides an excellent protecting
lead. Not only is it a safe lead, but it also offers a bare possibility that you may be able to trump the third round of Hearts.

6. LEAD 2 OF SPADES
The suit to lead is Spades.
Although Diamonds is your strongest suit, do not lead it. Avoid
opening any suit which was bid by your opponents unless you
hold a solid sequence in that suit. Although your 4-card Spade
suit headed by a single honor is not a desirable attacking lead,
it is the best lead you have, because all other suits were bid
by your opponents.
The card to lead is the 2.
Against a No trump contract lead fourth best, unless your
suit contains a leadable sequence.

QUIZ 6

1. **WHAT IS YOUR OPENING LEAD?**
   Your opponents' contract is 3 No trump.
   No suit was bid by your partner or your opponents.
   You are West. The bidding was as follows:

SOUTH	WEST	NORTH	EAST
1 No trump	Pass	2 No trump	Pass
3 No trump	Pass	Pass	Pass

2. **WHAT IS YOUR OPENING LEAD?**
   Your opponents' contract is 3 No trump.
   Your partner bid Hearts.
   You are West. The bidding was as follows:

EAST	SOUTH	WEST	NORTH
1 Heart	1 No trump	2 Hearts	2 No trump
Pass	3 No trump	Double	Pass
Pass	Pass		

3. **WHAT IS YOUR OPENING LEAD?**
   Your opponents' contract is 4 Spades.
   Your partner did not bid.
   You are West. The bidding was as follows:

SOUTH	WEST	NORTH	EAST
1 Spade	Pass	4 Spades	Pass
Pass	Pass		

4. **WHAT IS YOUR OPENING LEAD?**
   Your opponents' contract is 4 Spades.
   Your partner bid Hearts.
   You are West. The bidding was as follows:

NORTH	EAST	SOUTH	WEST
1 Diamond	1 Heart	1 Spade	2 Hearts
2 Spades	Pass	4 Spades	Pass
Pass	Pass		

ANSWERS

1. LEAD Q OF HEARTS
The suit to lead is Hearts.
A good attacking lead can be made by leading your Heart suit which is headed by an interrupted sequence. Do not lead your Club suit because it is headed by a high tenace.
The card to lead is the Q.
When you lead from a suit headed by a leadable sequence, always lead an honor instead of fourth best. Lead the highest honor in sequence.

2. LEAD Q OF HEARTS
The suit to lead is Hearts.
The heart suit is certainly the longest and strongest suit in your hand and your partner's hand combined.
The card to lead is the Q.
When you lead from a suit which was bid by your partner, in which you hold 2 honors in sequence or a leadable sequence, lead the highest honor in sequence.

3. LEAD Q OF HEARTS
The suit to lead is Hearts.
A lead from a 4-card or longer suit headed by an interrupted sequence is always a good attacking lead.
Do not lead Clubs. Avoid leading from a suit headed by a high tenace. Do not lead Spades. Even though you know that the dummy must be short in one of the side suits, it would be unwise to lead from a trump doubleton headed by a high honor.
The card to lead is the Q.
Whenever you lead from a suit headed by a leadable sequence, lead an honor instead of fourth best. Lead the highest of the 2 equal honors, unless they are the A K.

4. LEAD Q OF HEARTS
The suit to lead is Hearts.
Against a trump contract a lead from your partner's suit is a good attacking lead.
The card to lead is the Q.
Whenever you hold 2 touching honors (other than the A K) at the top of your partner's suit, lead the highest of the touching honors.

QUIZ 7

1. **WHAT IS YOUR OPENING LEAD?**
    Your opponents' contract is 3 No trump.
    Your partner bid Clubs.
    No suit was bid by either of your opponents.
    You are West. The bidding was as follows:

EAST	SOUTH	WEST	NORTH
1 Club	1 No trump	Pass	2 No trump
Pass	3 No trump	Pass	Pass
Pass			

2. **WHAT IS YOUR OPENING LEAD?**
    Your opponents' contract is 3 No trump.
    No suit was bid by your partner or your opponents.
    You are West. The bidding was as follows:

SOUTH	WEST	NORTH	EAST
1 No trump	Pass	2 No trump	Pass
3 No trump	Pass	Pass	Pass

3. **WHAT IS YOUR OPENING LEAD?**
    Your opponents' contract is 4 Spades.
    Your partner bid Clubs.
    You are West. The bidding was as follows:

EAST	SOUTH	WEST	NORTH
1 Club	2 Spades	Pass	3 Spades
Pass	4 Spades	Pass	Pass
Pass			

ANSWERS

1. **LEAD 10 OF CLUBS**
   The suit to lead is Clubs.
   Even if your partner has opened a short Club suit, which is likely, the longest and strongest suit in your combined hands is probably Clubs.
   You know that declarer holds at least 1 high Club. Otherwise he would not have bid No trump over your partner's opening bid of 1 Club. He may hold A J x or K J x. But even so, if you lead your 10 and hold back your Q, declarer's J can never take a trick, because your partner must hold either the A or the K.
   The card to lead is the 10.
   When you lead from a suit headed by a leadable sequence, always lead an honor instead of fourth best. When you lead from an intermediate sequence against a No trump contract, always lead the middle card of the sequence. Lead the higher of the 2 equal cards.

2. **LEAD 10 OF CLUBS**
   The suit to lead is Clubs.
   You have a difficult choice between Clubs and Hearts. A 4-card suit headed by an intermediate sequence is not a very desirable attacking lead and a 3-card suit headed J 10 is a preferred protecting lead. I would choose the Club lead.
   The card to lead is the 10.
   If you hold an intermediate sequence, against a No trump contract, always lead the honor which is in sequence with the next lower ranking card.

3. **LEAD 10 OF CLUBS**
   The suit to lead is Clubs.
   A lead from your partner's suit is a good attacking lead.
   The card to lead is the 10.
   If you hold a leadable sequence, always lead an honor instead of fourth best. When you lead from an intermediate sequence against a trump contract, lead the middle card in the sequence, unless you hold the A.

QUIZ 7 (continued)

4. **WHAT IS YOUR OPENING LEAD?**
   Your opponents' contract is 4 Spades.
   Your partner did not bid.
   You are West. The bidding was as follows:

SOUTH	WEST	NORTH	EAST
1 Spade	Pass	2 Diamonds	Pass
3 Spades	Pass	4 Spades	Pass
Pass	Pass		

5. **WHAT IS YOUR OPENING LEAD?**
   Your opponents' contract is 4 Spades.
   Your partner did not bid.
   You are West. The bidding was as follows:

SOUTH	WEST	NORTH	EAST
1 No trump	Pass	2 No trump	Pass
3 Spades	Pass	4 Spades	Pass
Pass	Pass		

6. **WHAT IS YOUR OPENING LEAD?**
   Your opponents' contract is 3 No trump.
   Your partner did not bid.
   You are West. The bidding was as follows:

SOUTH	WEST	NORTH	EAST
1 Spade	Pass	2 Hearts	Pass
2 No trump	Pass	3 Clubs	Pass
3 No trump	Pass	Pass	Pass

ANSWERS

4. LEAD J OF HEARTS
The suit to lead is Hearts.

No good attacking or ruffing lead is available. Do not lead Clubs. A 4-card suit headed by an intermediate sequence is not a desirable lead against a trump contract. Make a protecting lead.

A 3-card suit headed J 10 provides a good protecting lead. When you lead J from J 10 x, you do not run the risk of sacrificing a trick. If you happen to strike your partner's best suit, you will help establish it for him.

The card to lead is the J.

Always lead the highest honor from a 3-card suit headed by 2 equal honors.

5. LEAD 8 OF SPADES
The suit to lead is Spades.

You have no good attacking lead. Your only 4-card suit is headed by an intermediate sequence.

Although the J of Hearts would be a good protecting lead, the bidding has indicated that a trump lead would be better. Apparently both declarer and dummy each have 4 trumps. Make their trumps fall together to prevent a possible cross ruff.

The card to lead is the 8.

Lead the top of a worthless 3-card suit.°

6. LEAD 4 OF DIAMONDS
The suit to lead is Diamonds.

All suits have been bid by your opponents except Diamonds. A lead from a 3-card suit headed by only 1 honor usually is not recommended. However, in this case you should probably lead it, hoping that it is your partner's best suit.

The card to lead is the 4.

Against a No trump contract, always lead low from a 3-card suit headed by only 1 honor.

° Unless, before the game opened, your partner suggested that you lead low from a worthless 3-card suit, as some experts do.

QUIZ 8

1. WHAT IS YOUR OPENING LEAD?
Your opponents' contract is 2 No trump.
You bid 1 Heart.
Your partner bid Spades.
Your partner raised your Hearts.
You are West. The bidding was as follows:

WEST	NORTH	EAST	SOUTH
1 Heart	Pass	1 Spade	1 No trump
Pass	Pass	2 Hearts	2 No trump
Double	Pass	Pass	Pass

2. WHAT IS YOUR OPENING LEAD?
Your opponents' contract is 4 Spades.
Your partner bid Clubs.
You are West. The bidding was as follows:

EAST	SOUTH	WEST	NORTH
1 Club	4 Spades	Double	Pass
Pass	Pass		

3. WHAT IS YOUR OPENING LEAD?
Your opponents' contract is 2 Clubs.
Your partner did not bid.
You are West. The bidding was as follows:

SOUTH	WEST	NORTH	EAST
1 Club	Pass	1 Heart	Pass
2 Clubs	Pass	Pass	Pass

ANSWERS

1. **LEAD 4 OF HEARTS**
   The suit to lead is Hearts.
   Lead your own Heart suit instead of your partner's Spades, because your partner raised your Hearts. You have poor support for your partner's Spades.
   The card to lead is the 4.
   Always lead fourth best against a No trump contract, when you do not have a leadable sequence.

2. **LEAD A OF CLUBS**
   The suit to lead is Clubs.
   A lead from your partner's suit is always a good attacking lead. Do not lead Hearts or Diamonds. Avoid a 4-card suit headed by 1 honor or by 2 honors not in sequence. Do not lead trumps when you have a good attacking lead.
   The card to lead is the A.
   When you lead your partner's suit lead the A, if the lead is against a trump contract.

3. **LEAD 6 OF SPADES**
   The suit to lead is Spades.
   No good attacking lead is available. Do not lead Diamonds. Avoid a 4-card suit headed by a single honor. Hearts, of course, is the worst possible lead.
   A lead from a low doubleton is a good protecting lead. Moreover, in this case, since you can stop the trump lead twice, you have a very good chance to ruff the third round of Spades with your 2 of Clubs.
   The card to lead is the 6.
   From a doubleton, always lead the highest card.

QUIZ 8 (continued)

4. **WHAT IS YOUR OPENING LEAD?**
   Your opponents' contract is 3 No trump.
   Your partner doubled.
   Your partner did not bid a suit.
   You bid Hearts.
   You are West. The bidding was as follows:

WEST	NORTH	EAST	SOUTH
1 Heart	Double	Pass	1 No trump
Pass	3 No trump	Double	Pass
Pass	Pass		

5. **WHAT IS YOUR OPENING LEAD?**
   Your opponents' contract is 1 Spade doubled.
   You are West. The bidding was as follows:

SOUTH	WEST	NORTH	EAST
1 Spade	Double	Pass	Pass
Pass			

6. **WHAT IS YOUR OPENING LEAD?**
   Your opponents' contract is 3 Spades.
   Your partner bid Clubs.
   You are West. The bidding was as follows:

SOUTH	WEST	NORTH	EAST
1 Spade	Double	Pass	2 Clubs
3 Spades	Pass	Pass	Pass

ANSWERS

4. LEAD 4 OF HEARTS
The suit to lead is Hearts.

Against a No trump contract which your partner has doubled (if you have bid a suit, but your partner has not bid) lead the suit you bid. Your partner's double is a lead-directing signal.

The card to lead is the 4.

When you lead a suit which was not bid by your partner, always lead fourth best against a No trump contract, unless you have a leadable sequence.

5. LEAD 6 OF SPADES
The suit to lead is Spades.

If you have made a takeout double, and your partner passes, allowing the double to stand instead of taking it out, you know that he has great length and strength in the trump suit. Such a penalty pass by your partner invites you to lead trumps. Unless you can make a strong attacking lead, you should lead trumps.

The card to lead is the 6.

Always lead the highest card from a doubleton.

6. LEAD 6 OF SPADES
The suit to lead is Spades.

In spite of the fact that your partner bid Clubs, you cannot count on him for any high cards in that suit. Your takeout double forced him to bid. He might possibly hold only 4 small Clubs. So do not lead from your A Q tenace.

Neither your Hearts nor Diamonds provides a good attacking lead.

The only protecting lead you can make is a trump lead.

The card to lead is the 6.

Lead the highest card from any doubleton.

QUIZ 9

1. WHAT IS YOUR OPENING LEAD?
Your opponents' contract is 3 No trump.
Your partner bid Diamonds.
You are West. The bidding was as follows:

NORTH	EAST	SOUTH	WEST
1 Club	1 Diamond	1 No trump	Pass
3 No trump	Pass	Pass	Pass

2. WHAT IS YOUR OPENING LEAD?
Your opponents' contract is 3 Hearts.
Your partner bid Spades.
You are West. The bidding was as follows:

SOUTH	WEST	NORTH	EAST
1 Heart	Pass	Pass	1 Spade
3 Hearts	Pass	Pass	Pass

3. WHAT IS YOUR OPENING LEAD?
Your opponents' contract is 4 Hearts.
Your partner did not bid.
Your are West. The bidding was as follows:

SOUTH	WEST	NORTH	EAST
1 Heart	Pass	2 Hearts	Pass
4 Hearts	Pass	Pass	Pass

4. WHAT IS YOUR OPENING LEAD?
Your opponents' contract is 3 Clubs.
Your partner did not bid.
You are West. The bidding was as follows:

SOUTH	WEST	NORTH	EAST
1 Club	Pass	2 Clubs	Pass
3 Clubs	Pass	Pass	Pass

ANSWERS

1. **LEAD 7 OF DIAMONDS**
   The suit to lead is Diamonds.
   You have no long, strong suit of your own. Your partner's Diamond suit is obviously the suit to lead. Do not lead Spades. Avoid a 4-card suit headed by only 1 honor.
   The card to lead is the 7.
   When you hold 3 cards in your partner's suit headed by only 1 honor, always lead the lowest card against a No trump contract.

2. **LEAD A OF SPADES**
   The suit to lead is Spades.
   A lead from your partner's suit is always a good attacking lead.
   The card to lead is the A.
   If you hold the A of your partner's suit, always lead the A against a trump contract.

3. **LEAD 6 OF CLUBS**
   The suit to lead is Clubs.
   Do not lead Spades. Avoid a 4-card suit headed by only 1 honor.
   When no good attacking or ruffing lead is available, make a protecting lead. A good protecting lead is a lead from a worthless 3-card suit.
   The card to lead is the 6.
   From a worthless 3-card suit, lead the highest card.°

4. **LEAD 6 OF CLUBS**
   The suit to lead is Clubs.
   No good attacking lead is available. Do not lead Spades. A 4-card suit headed by a single honor is not a good attacking lead.
   When you hold 2 or 3 small trumps, a lead of trumps is an acceptable protecting lead, if no other good lead is available. Do not lead Hearts or Diamonds. A 3-card suit headed by a single honor is not a good protecting lead.
   The card to lead is the 6.
   When you lead from a 3-card suit without any honors, always lead the highest card.°

° Unless, before the game opened, your partner suggested that you lead low from a worthless 3-card suit, as some experts do.

QUIZ 10

1. WHAT IS YOUR OPENING LEAD?

Your opponents' contract is 3 No trump.
Your partner bid Spades.
You are West. The bidding was as follows:

NORTH	EAST	SOUTH	WEST
1 Club	1 Spade	2 No trump	Pass
3 No trump	Pass	Pass	Pass

2. WHAT IS YOUR OPENING LEAD?

Your opponents' contract is 3 No trump.
Your partner doubled.
Your partner bid Spades.
You are West. The bidding was as follows:

NORTH	EAST	SOUTH	WEST
1 Club	1 Spade	2 No trump	Pass
3 No trump	Double	Pass	Pass
Pass			

3. WHAT IS YOUR OPENING LEAD?

Your opponents' contract is 4 Spades.
Your partner bid Hearts.
You are West. The bidding was as follows:

NORTH	EAST	SOUTH	WEST
1 Club	1 Heart	4 Spades	Pass
Pass	Pass		

4. WHAT IS YOUR OPENING LEAD?

Your opponents' contract is 4 Hearts.
Your partner bid Spades.
You are West. The bidding was as follows:

NORTH	EAST	SOUTH	WEST
1 Club	1 Spade	3 Hearts	Pass
4 Hearts	Pass	Pass	Pass

ANSWERS

1. **LEAD K OF DIAMONDS**
      The suit to lead is Diamonds.
   Lead your own suit instead of your partner's, if you have a singleton in your partner's suit and a strong suit of your own. Although your Diamond suit has only 4 cards, it is very strong.
      The card to lead is the K.
   Always lead your highest card from a solid sequence of honors.

2. **LEAD 4 OF SPADES**
      The suit to lead is Spades.
   Whenever your partner doubles a No trump contract, if he has bid a suit and you have not, lead your partner's suit. His double is a lead-directing signal which should be obeyed.

3. **LEAD K OF DIAMONDS**
      The suit to lead is Diamonds.
   A lead from a 4-card or longer suit headed by a solid sequence is always a good attacking lead. It is better to lead from such a suit than to lead your partner's suit. Moreover, the first lead of Hearts might well be trumped, because your partner probably has at least 5 Hearts and you have 4.
      The card to lead is the K.
   When you lead from a suit headed by a solid sequence, always lead the highest honor.

4. **LEAD K OF DIAMONDS**
      The suit to lead is Diamonds.
   Against a trump contract, if you have 4 or more trumps, lead the suit you would open against a No trump contract. This suit is Diamonds. Establish your Diamond suit immediately and lead it at every opportunity to make declarer use one of his long trumps to stop your Diamonds. You may weaken his trump suit so much that he will not be able to draw all your trumps. You will probably gain more in this way than you would gain by trumping Spades.
      The card to lead is the K.
   Always lead the highest honor when you hold a solid sequence.

QUIZ 11

1. WHAT IS YOUR OPENING LEAD?

Your opponents' contract is 3 No trump.

Your partner did not bid.

You are West. The bidding was as follows:

NORTH	EAST	SOUTH	WEST
1 Club	Pass	2 No trump	Pass
3 No trump	Pass	Pass	Pass

2. WHAT IS YOUR OPENING LEAD?

Your opponents' contract is 4 Hearts.

Your partner did not bid.

You are West. The bidding was as follows:

SOUTH	WEST	NORTH	EAST
1 Hearts	1 Spade	2 Hearts	Pass
4 Hearts	Pass	Pass	Pass

3. WHAT IS YOUR OPENING LEAD?

Your opponents' contract is 3 No trump.

Your partner did not bid.

Dummy bid Spades.

You are West. The bidding was as follows:

NORTH	EAST	SOUTH	WEST
1 Spade	Pass	2 No trump	Pass
3 No trump	Pass	Pass	Pass

4. WHAT IS YOUR OPENING LEAD?

Your opponents' contract is 3 No trump.

Your partner bid Clubs.

You are West. The bidding was as follows:

NORTH	EAST	SOUTH	WEST
1 Heart	2 Clubs	2 No trump	Pass
3 No trump	Pass	Pass	Pass

ANSWERS

1. **LEAD J OF SPADES**
   The suit to lead is Spades.
   Since your partner did not bid, lead your own longest suit.
   The card to lead is the J.
   From an intermediate sequence, always lead the highest of the 2 equal cards against a No trump contract.

2. **LEAD 8 OF CLUBS**
   The suit to lead is Clubs.
   Do not lead a Spade, because a lead from a 4-card or longer suit headed by an intermediate sequence is not a good attacking lead against a trump contract. A good protecting lead is a lead from a 3-card suit without any honors.
   The card to lead is the 8.
   When you lead from a worthless 3-card suit, always lead the highest card.°

3. **LEAD 8 OF CLUBS**
   The suit to lead is Clubs.
   Your only long suit is Spades, but it was bid by your opponents. So do not lead it. Make a protecting short suit lead.
   Do not lead from a high doubleton. A good protecting lead is a lead from a 3-card suit, provided it is not headed by 1 honor or 2 honors not in sequence.
   The card to lead is the 8.
   When you lead from a 3-card suit without any honors, always lead the highest card.°

4. **LEAD 8 OF CLUBS**
   The suit to lead is Clubs.
   You can not be sure that your partner's Clubs are stronger than your Spades. But whenever you are in doubt, lead your partner's suit instead of your own against a No trump contract.
   The card to lead is the 8.
   When you lead from a worthless 3-card suit, always lead the highest card.°

° Some expert players lead the lowest card from a worthless 3-card suit. But unless you and your partner have previously agreed to lead low from such a suit, you should lead "top of nothing."

QUIZ 12

1. WHAT IS YOUR OPENING LEAD?

Your opponents' contract is 3 No trump.
Your partner bid Hearts.
You are West. The bidding was as follows:

NORTH	EAST	SOUTH	WEST
1 Diamond	1 Heart	1 No trump	2 Clubs
2 No trump	Pass	3 No trump	Double
Pass	Pass	Pass	

2. WHAT IS YOUR OPENING LEAD?

Your opponents' contract is 3 No trump.
Your partner did not bid.
Dummy bid Clubs.
You are West. The bidding was as follows:

NORTH	EAST	SOUTH	WEST
1 Club	Pass	2 No trump	Pass
3 No trump	Pass	Pass	Double
Pass	Pass	Pass	

3. WHAT IS YOUR OPENING LEAD?

Your opponents' contract is 4 Hearts.
Your partner did not bid.
You are West. The bidding was as follows:

SOUTH	WEST	NORTH	EAST
1 Heart	2 Clubs	2 Spades	Pass
3 Hearts	Pass	4 Hearts	Pass
Pass	Pass		

ANSWERS

1. **LEAD Q OF CLUBS**
    The suit to lead is Clubs.
    Against a No trump contract, as a general rule, lead your partner's suit in preference to your own. However, lead your own suit instead of your partner's, if you have a long, solid suit and enough entries to defeat the contract without help from your partner.
    Two leads of Clubs will establish your Club suit. With two sure entries you will be able to regain the lead and set the contract by cashing your remaining Clubs.
    The card to lead is the Q.
    When you lead from a solid sequence not headed by the A, always lead the highest honor.

2. **LEAD Q OF CLUBS**
    The suit to lead is Clubs.
    In spite of the fact that dummy bid your suit, lead Clubs because your suit is headed by a solid sequence. Your opponents can stop the Club suit only twice. After that your small Clubs will take enough tricks to set the contract.
    The card to lead is the Q.
    Against a No trump contract, when you lead from a 4-card or longer suit headed by a leadable sequence, lead an honor instead of fourth best. When you lead an honor, lead the highest honor in sequence.

3. **LEAD Q OF CLUBS**
    The suit to lead is Clubs.
    Against a trump contract a good attacking lead is a lead from a 4-card or longer suit headed by a solid sequence.
    The card to lead is the Q.
    From a solid sequence headed K, Q, J, or 10, always lead the highest card.

QUIZ 12 (continued)

4. **WHAT IS YOUR OPENING LEAD?**
   Your opponents' contract is 4 Diamonds.
   Your partner bid Spades.
   You are West. The bidding was as follows:

NORTH	EAST	SOUTH	WEST
1 Heart	1 Spade	2 Diamonds	2 Spades
3 Diamonds	Pass	4 Diamonds	Pass

5. **WHAT IS YOUR OPENING LEAD?**
   Your opponents' contract is 1 Heart doubled.
   You are West. The bidding was as follows:

SOUTH	WEST	NORTH	EAST
1 Heart	Double	Pass	Pass
Pass			

6. **WHAT IS YOUR OPENING LEAD?**
   Your opponents' contract is 3 Hearts.
   Your partner did not bid.
   You are West. The bidding was as follows:

SOUTH	WEST	NORTH	EAST
1 Club	Pass	1 Spade	Pass
2 Hearts	Pass	3 Hearts	Pass
4 Hearts	Pass	Pass	Pass

ANSWERS

4. **LEAD J OF SPADES**
   The suit to lead is Spades.
   A lead from your partner's suit is always a good attacking lead.
   The card to lead is the J.
   When you lead from an intermediate sequence in your partner's suit, always lead the middle card in the sequence, unless you can lead the A against a trump contract.

5. **LEAD Q OF CLUBS**
   The suit to lead is Clubs.
   If you have made a takeout double, and your partner passes, allowing the double to stand instead of taking it out, you know that your partner has great length and strength in the trump suit. Such a penalty pass invites you to lead trumps. However, if you have a strong attacking lead which will not risk the loss of a high card, it is better to make the attacking lead.
   The card to lead is the Q.
   When you lead from a suit headed by a solid sequence, lead the highest card, unless your sequence is A K Q.

6. **LEAD 7 OF HEARTS**
   The suit to lead is Hearts.
   It is very probable that dummy is short in Clubs, since you have 6 Clubs and declarer must have at least 3. In that event declarer will plan to ruff losing Clubs with dummy's trumps. Therefore lead trumps immediately.
   The card to lead is the 7.
   Always lead the highest card from a doubleton.

QUIZ 13

1. WHAT IS YOUR OPENING LEAD?

Your opponents' contract is 3 No trump.
No suit was bid by your partner or your opponents.
You are West. The bidding was as follows:

SOUTH	WEST	NORTH	EAST
1 No trump	Pass	2 No trump	Pass
3 No trump	Pass	Pass	Pass

2. WHAT IS YOUR OPENING LEAD?

Your opponents' contract is 5 Clubs.
Your partner bid Diamonds.
You are West. The bidding was as follows:

NORTH	EAST	SOUTH	WEST
1 Heart	2 Diamonds	4 Clubs	Pass
5 Clubs	Pass	Pass	Pass

3. WHAT IS YOUR OPENING LEAD?

Your opponents' contract is 2 Diamonds.
Your partner did not bid.
You are West. The bidding was as follows:

SOUTH	WEST	NORTH	EAST
1 Diamond	Pass	2 Diamonds	Pass
Pass	Pass		

4. WHAT IS YOUR OPENING LEAD?

Your opponents' contract is 2 Spades.
Your partner did not bid.
You are West. The bidding was as follows:

SOUTH	WEST	NORTH	EAST
1 Spade	Pass	2 Diamonds	Pass
2 Spades	Pass	Pass	Pass

ANSWERS

4. LEAD 7 OF DIAMONDS
  The suit to lead is Diamonds.
You have no good attacking lead, so you must choose a pro-
tecting lead. Do not lead Clubs, because dummy bid Clubs.
Your choice lies between Diamonds and Spades.
  Against a trump contract a doubleton offers a good pro-
tecting lead. You have 2 "extra" trumps. There is a bare
chance that you will be able to trump a Diamond.
  The card to lead is the 7.
From a doubleton, always lead the highest card.

5. LEAD 2 OF CLUBS
  The suit to lead is Clubs.
When your partner doubles your opponents' response to a
Blackwood 4 No trump bid, his double is a lead-directing
signal. Your partner's double suggests that you lead the suit
he doubled.
  The card to lead is the 2.
When you lead from a 4-card or longer suit, as a general
rule lead fourth best.

6. LEAD 2 OF SPADES
  The suit to lead is Spades.
When dummy responded 5 Clubs after declarer's Blackwood
4 No trump bid, your partner passed. He did not make a
lead-directing double. Therefore, you can assume that he
has no desire to have you lead Clubs. So lead Spades rather
than Clubs.
  Do not lead Diamonds, because that suit was bid by the
dummy.
  The card to lead is the 2.
Against a trump contract lead fourth best, unless you hold the
A or 2 honors in sequence or a leadable sequence.

QUIZ 15

1. WHAT IS YOUR OPENING LEAD?
Your opponents' contract is 3 No trump.
Your partner did not bid.
You are West. The bidding was as follows:

SOUTH	WEST	NORTH	EAST
1 No trump	Pass	2 No trump	Pass
3 No trump	Pass	Pass	Pass

2. WHAT IS YOUR OPENING LEAD?
Your opponents' contract is 4 Hearts.
You bid 1 Diamond.
Your partner raised your Diamonds.
You are West. The bidding was as follows:

WEST	NORTH	EAST	SOUTH
1 Diamond	1 Spade	2 Diamonds	2 Hearts
Pass	3 Hearts	Pass	4 Hearts
Pass	Pass		

3. WHAT IS YOUR OPENING LEAD?
Your opponents' contract is 4 Hearts.
Your partner did not bid.
You are West. The bidding was as follows:

SOUTH	WEST	NORTH	EAST
2 Hearts	Pass	2 No trump	Pass
4 Hearts	Pass	Pass	Pass

4. WHAT IS YOUR OPENING LEAD?
Your opponents' contract is 2 Spades.
Your partner did not bid.
You are West. The bidding was as follows:

SOUTH	WEST	NORTH	EAST
1 Spade	Pass	2 Spades	Pass
Pass	Pass		

ANSWERS

1. **LEAD 2 OF CLUBS**
   The suit to lead is Clubs.
   Here you have a choice of evils. There is no good attacking
   or protecting lead in your hand, and there was nothing in
   the bidding to help you decide. Perhaps the least harmful
   lead you can make is Clubs.
   The card to lead is the 2.
   Against a No trump contract, lead fourth best, unless you
   hold a leadable sequence.

2. **LEAD A OF DIAMONDS**
   The suit to lead is Diamonds.
   A lead from a suit you bid and which your partner raised
   is a good attacking lead no matter how your suit is headed.
   The card to lead is the A.
   Against a trump contract, when leading from a 4-card or
   longer suit headed by the A, lead the A instead of fourth best.

3. **LEAD 8 OF HEARTS**
   The suit to lead is Hearts.
   You have no good attacking or ruffing lead.
   You have a choice between 2 possible protecting leads,
   Spades and Hearts. Neither of them is desirable. A Spade
   lead would probably sacrifice a trick, because declarer prob-
   ably holds the A of Spades. Therefore open from your
   trump doubleton.
   The card to lead is the 8.
   When leading from a doubleton, always lead the highest
   card.

4. **LEAD 8 OF HEARTS**
   The suit to lead is Hearts.
   Your partner did not bid, and you have no good attacking
   or ruffing lead. Do not lead Diamonds or Clubs. Avoid a 4-
   card suit headed by 1 honor or by a high tenace.
   A lead from your low doubleton is a good protecting lead.
   The card to lead is the 8.
   Always lead the highest card from a doubleton.

QUIZ 16

1. WHAT IS YOUR OPENING LEAD?
Your opponents' contract is 4 Hearts.
Your partner bid Spades.
You are West. The bidding was as follows:

NORTH	EAST	SOUTH	WEST
1 Diamond	1 Spade	2 Hearts	2 Spades
3 Hearts	Pass	4 Hearts	Pass
Pass	Pass		

2. WHAT IS YOUR OPENING LEAD?
Your opponents' contract is 4 Spades.
Your partner did not bid.
You are West. The bidding was as follows:

SOUTH	WEST	NORTH	EAST
1 Spade	Pass	2 Spades	Pass
4 Spades	Pass	Pass	Pass

3. WHAT IS YOUR OPENING LEAD?
Your opponents' contract is 4 Hearts.
Your partner did not bid.
You are West. The bidding was as follows:

SOUTH	WEST	NORTH	EAST
1 Heart	Pass	2 Hearts	Pass
4 Hearts	Pass	Pass	Pass

4. WHAT IS YOUR OPENING LEAD?
Your opponents' contract is 3 No trump.
Your partner bid Diamonds.
You are West. The bidding was as follows:

NORTH	EAST	SOUTH	WEST
1 Spade	2 Diamonds	2 No trump	Pass
3 No trump	Pass	Pass	Pass

ANSWERS

1. LEAD 2 OF DIAMONDS
The suit to lead is Diamonds.

You have all the requirements for a lead of a singleton in a suit which was not bid by your partner.

You hold not more than 3 trumps, including an extra trump. You have a stopper in trumps. Your partner has bid, indicating that he probably has an entry in Spades.

2. LEAD A OF CLUBS
The suit to lead is Clubs.

Do not lead your singleton Diamond. If you have 4 or more trumps, lead the suit you would open against a No trump contract.

Against a No trump contract you would lead the suit which is probably the longest and strongest in your hand and your partner's hand combined. Since your partner did not bid, you would lead your own longest and strongest suit. Try to establish your Club suit and force the declarer to trump, so he will exhaust his trumps.

The card to lead is the A.

Against a trump contract, when you lead from a 4-card or longer suit headed by the A, always lead the A instead of fourth best.

3. LEAD 2 OF SPADES
The suit to lead is Spades.

No good attacking lead is available. The singleton Diamond is not a good ruffing lead, because your partner did not bid and you can not count on him for an entry.

Therefore, make a protecting lead. A good protecting lead is a lead from a worthless 4-card suit.

The card to lead is the 2.

When you lead from 4 or more small cards, always lead fourth best.

4. LEAD 2 OF DIAMONDS
The suit to lead is Diamonds.

Against a No trump contract, as a general rule, lead the suit which is probably the longest and strongest in your hand and your partner's hand combined. You do not have a long, strong suit of your own, so lead your partner's suit even though you have only a singleton in his suit.

QUIZ 17

1. WHAT IS YOUR OPENING LEAD?

Your opponents' contract is 4 Spades.
Your partner bid Diamonds.
You are West. The bidding was as follows:

NORTH	EAST	SOUTH	WEST
1 Club	1 Diamond	2 Spades	Pass
3 Spades	Pass	4 Spades	Pass
Pass	Pass		

2. WHAT IS YOUR OPENING LEAD?

Your opponents' contract is 4 Spades.
Your partner did not bid.
You are West. The bidding was as follows:

SOUTH	WEST	NORTH	EAST
1 Spade	Pass	3 Spades	Pass
4 Spades	Pass	Pass	Pass

3. WHAT IS YOUR OPENING LEAD?

Your opponents' contract is 3 No trump.
Your partner bid Spades.
You are West. The bidding was as follows:

NORTH	EAST	SOUTH	WEST
1 Club	1 Spade	1 No trump	Pass
3 No trump	Pass	Pass	Pass

4. WHAT IS YOUR OPENING LEAD?

Your opponents' contract is 3 No trump.
Your partner doubled.
Your partner did not bid a suit.
You are West. The bidding was as follows:

SOUTH	WEST	NORTH	EAST
1 Spade	Pass	2 Diamonds	Pass
3 No trump	Pass	Pass	Double
Pass	Pass	Pass	

ANSWERS

1. **LEAD A OF CLUBS**
   The suit to lead is Clubs.
   You hold not more than 3 trumps. All of them are "extra" trumps. Your partner has bid, indicating that he has an entry. Under these conditions the lead of a singleton A is a good ruffing lead, even though you do not have a stopper in the trump suit.

2. **LEAD 8 OF DIAMONDS**
   The suit to lead is Diamonds.
   No good attacking lead is available. The singleton A of Clubs is not a good ruffing lead, because your partner did not bid and you can not count on him for an entry.
   You have a choice between 2 good protecting leads, Diamonds and Spades. Diamonds is the better choice. Trumps should not usually be led if another good protecting lead is available.
   The card to lead is the 8.
   When you lead from a 3-card suit without an honor, lead the highest card.°

3. **LEAD 7 OF SPADES**
   The suit to lead is Spades.
   Against a No trump contract, as a general rule, lead the suit which is probably the longest and strongest in your hand and your partner's hand combined. If your partner has bid, usually lead your partner's suit instead of your own.
   The card to lead is the 7.
   Always lead the highest of 3 small cards.°

4. **LEAD 8 OF DIAMONDS**
   The suit to lead is Diamonds.
   Neither you nor your partner has bid. Nevertheless, your partner's double of a No trump contract is a lead-directing signal. He asks you to lead the Diamond suit which dummy bid but did not rebid and which declarer did not raise.
   The card to lead is the 8.
   When you lead from a worthless 3-card suit, always lead the highest card.°

° Some top-ranking players prefer to lead the lowest card from a worthless 3-card suit. But lead your highest card if your partner has not specifically suggested that you lead low from such a suit.

QUIZ 18

1. WHAT IS YOUR OPENING LEAD?

Your opponents' contract is 4 Spades.
Your partner bid Clubs.
You are West. The bidding was as follows:

NORTH	EAST	SOUTH	WEST
1 Heart	2 Clubs	2 Spades	3 Clubs
3 Spades	Pass	4 Spades	Pass
Pass	Pass		

2. WHAT IS YOUR OPENING LEAD?

Your opponents' contract is 4 Spades.
Your partner did not bid.
You are West. The bidding was as follows:

SOUTH	WEST	NORTH	EAST
1 Spade	Pass	2 Diamonds	Pass
3 Spades	Pass	4 Spades	Pass
Pass	Pass		

3. WHAT IS YOUR OPENING LEAD?

Your opponents' contract is 3 No trump.
Your partner did not bid.
You are West. The bidding was as follows:

NORTH	EAST	SOUTH	WEST
1 Club	Pass	1 Spade	Pass
3 Clubs	Pass	3 No trump	Pass
Pass	Pass		

4. WHAT IS YOUR OPENING LEAD?

Your opponents' contract is 2 Clubs.
Your partner did not bid.
You are West. The bidding was as follows:

SOUTH	WEST	NORTH	EAST
1 Club	Pass	1 Spade	Pass
2 Clubs	Pass	Pass	Pass

ANSWERS

1. **LEAD A OF DIAMONDS AND FOLLOW WITH THE K**
   The suit to lead is Diamonds.
   You have a good ruffing lead. You hold not more than 3 trumps, all of them "extra" trumps. Your partner has bid, indicating that he has an entry. Lead the doubleton A K, even though you do not have a stopper in trumps.
   The card to lead is the A.
   When you lead from a doubleton, even a doubleton A K, always lead the highest card.

2. **LEAD 2 OF CLUBS**
   The suit to lead is Clubs.
   No good attacking lead is available. The doubleton A K of Diamonds is not a good ruffing lead, because your partner did not bid and you can not count on him for an entry.
   Therefore choose between the 2 protecting leads you have available, Clubs and Spades. A worthless 3- or 4-card suit should perhaps be chosen rather than trumps.
   The card to lead is the 2.
   Always lead fourth best from a worthless 4-card suit.

3. **LEAD 3 OF HEARTS**
   The suit to lead is Hearts.
   Even though your Heart suit is only 4 cards and is headed by only 1 honor, a Heart lead is the least objectionable lead available.
   The card to lead is the 3.
   When you lead a 4-card or longer suit against a No trump contract, always lead fourth best, unless the suit is headed by a leadable sequence.

4. **LEAD 3 OF HEARTS**
   The suit to lead is Hearts.
   Against a trump contract, if you have 4 or more trumps, lead the suit you would open against a No trump contract.
   The card to lead is the 3.
   When you lead from a 4-card or longer suit, as a general rule, lead fourth best.

QUIZ 19

1. **WHAT IS YOUR OPENING LEAD?**
   Your opponents' contract is 3 No trump.
   Your partner bid Clubs.
   You are West. The bidding was as follows:

NORTH	EAST	SOUTH	WEST
1 Spade	2 Clubs	2 No trump	Pass
3 No trump	Pass	Pass	Pass

2. **WHAT IS YOUR OPENING LEAD?**
   Your opponents' contract is 3 Diamonds.
   Your partner bid Clubs.
   You are West. The bidding was as follows:

NORTH	EAST	SOUTH	WEST
1 Spade	2 Clubs	2 Diamonds	Pass
2 Hearts	Pass	3 Diamonds	Pass
Pass	Pass		

3. **WHAT IS YOUR OPENING LEAD?**
   Your opponents' contract is 3 No trump.
   Your partner did not bid.
   You are West. The bidding was as follows:

SOUTH	WEST	NORTH	EAST
1 No trump	Pass	2 No trump	Pass
3 No trump	Pass	Pass	Pass

4. **WHAT IS YOUR OPENING LEAD?**
   Your opponents' contract is 3 No trump.
   Your partner did not bid.
   You are West. The bidding was as follows:

SOUTH	WEST	NORTH	EAST
1 Club	Pass	1 Spade	Pass
2 No trump	Pass	3 No trump	Pass
Pass	Pass		

ANSWERS

1. **LEAD J OF CLUBS**
   The suit to lead is Clubs.
   There can be no question about which suit to lead.
   The card to lead is the J.
   Against a No trump contract, when you lead from a suit headed by an intermediate sequence, always lead the middle card in the sequence, the higher of the 2 equal cards.

2. **LEAD J OF CLUBS**
   The suit to lead is Clubs.
   Your partner's suit always is a good attacking lead.
   The card to lead is the J.
   Against a trump contract, when you lead from a suit headed by an intermediate sequence, lead the middle card in the sequence, unless the suit is headed by the A.

3. **LEAD 2 OF SPADES**
   The suit to lead is Spades.
   Your longest and strongest suit is Clubs. But if you lead your J of Clubs your opponents will almost surely take the first trick with the Q. Wait until Clubs are led up to you. Then if declarer holds the Q, his Q will never take a trick.
   You have a choice of 2 good protecting leads, Spades and Hearts. The Spades may turn out best.
   The card to lead is the 2.
   Lead fourth best against a No trump unless you have a leadable sequence.

4. **LEAD J OF HEARTS**
   The suit to lead is Hearts.
   No good attacking lead is available. Do not lead Clubs or Spades, because your opponents bid these suits.
   When you choose a protecting lead against No trump, avoid a doubleton if you have any other protecting lead. A 3-card suit headed J 10 is a good protecting lead.
   The card to lead is the J.
   When you lead from a 3-card suit, headed by 2 honors in sequence other than A K, always lead the highest card.

QUIZ 20

1. **WHAT IS YOUR OPENING LEAD?**
   Your opponents' contract is 1 No trump.
   Your partner did not bid.
   You are West. The bidding was as follows:

SOUTH	WEST	NORTH	EAST
1 No trump	Pass	Pass	Pass

2. **WHAT CARD DO YOU PLAY?**
   Your opponents' contract is 4 Hearts.
   When trumps are led, what card will you play?

3. **WHAT CARD DO YOU PLAY?**
   Your opponents' contract is 5 Clubs.
   When trumps are led, what card will you play?

4. **WHAT CARD DO YOU PLAY?**
   Your opponents' contract is 4 Hearts.
   Your partner led the 5 of Spades.

5. **WHAT CARD DO YOU PLAY?**
   Your opponents' contract is 5 Clubs.
   Your partner led the 5 of Spades.

ANSWERS

1. **LEAD A OF DIAMONDS**
   The suit to lead is Diamonds.
   This is obvious.
   The card to lead is the A.
   Against a No trump contract, if you have a long, powerful suit which is solid or almost solid, lead the A and follow up by leading the K and Q with the hope that the J will fall.
   When you lead the A, you tell your partner that you have a long, powerful suit that is solid or almost solid. You ask him to unblock.

2. **PLAY 2 OF HEARTS**
   If you hold only 2 trumps, follow suit with your lowest trump, even though there is a suit you want to ruff.
   If you were to play the 6 first and later the 2, your partner would think that you still hold another trump. A high-low trump echo the first and second time you play a trump is used to signal your partner only when all three of the following conditions prevail:
   1. You hold at least 3 trumps.
   2. You are void in a suit.
   3. You can spare one of your trumps to ruff the suit in which you are blank.

3. **PLAY 5 OF CLUBS**
   You hold more than 2 trumps and there is a suit you want to ruff. You can give your partner this information by following suit first with a trump which is not your lowest, and next with your lowest trump.

4. **PLAY 2 OF HEARTS**
   If you hold only 2 trumps, ruff with your lowest trump. If you were to ruff first with your 6 and then later with your 2, your trump echo would lead your partner to believe that you still have a trump left with which to ruff a third time, if the suit can be led again.

5. **PLAY 5 OF CLUBS**
   You hold more than 2 trumps. If you ruff first with your 5 and later play your 4, your partner will know that you still have a trump left with which you can ruff again.

QUIZ 21

YOUR PARTNER'S HAND

DECLARER'S HAND

DUMMY

♠ 2 ♠ 3 ♠ 6 ♠ A
♡ 4 ♡ K
♣ 7 ♣ 9 ♣ J
♦ 6 ♦ 7 ♦ 9 ♦ 10

♠ J ♠ 4 ♡ J ♡ 10 ♡ 2 ♣ 10 ♣ 8 ♣ 3 ♣ 2 ♦ A ♦ K ♦ 8 ♦ 4

YOUR OWN HAND

1. **WHAT CARD DO YOU PLAY?**
   Your opponents' contract is 4 Spades.
   Your partner's opening lead is A of Hearts.

2. **WHAT CARD DO YOU PLAY?**
   Your opponents' contract is 2 Spades.
   Your partner's opening lead is A of Clubs.

3. **WHAT DOES YOUR PARTNER'S LEAD TELL YOU?**
   Your opponents' contract is 4 Spades.
   Neither you nor your partner bid.
   Your partner's opening lead is 3 of Diamonds.

ANSWERS

1. **PLAY J OF HEARTS**
    When your partner studies the dummy, he will recognize that you are not giving him a conventional "come-on" signal asking him to continue to lead Hearts. He will realize that you are giving him a suit-preference signal. There are only 2 other suits which you might want him to lead — Diamonds and Clubs.
    If you play a high card on the first trick, you tell him to lead the higher ranking of these 2 suits, which is Diamonds.

2. **PLAY 2 OF CLUBS**
    When you follow suit with your lowest card, you give your partner a warning signal asking him not to lead that suit again.

3. **YOUR PARTNER PROBABLY IS LEADING FROM A DOUBLETON**
    Your partner is not leading fourth best.
    By subtracting 3 from 11 you know that there would be only 8 cards higher than the 3 outside your partner's hand, if your partner's lead were fourth best. You can count 8 higher cards in your own hand and the dummy. Therefore, if your partner's lead were fourth best your partner would hold both the Q and J. In this case he would lead the Q instead of the 3.
    Your partner probably is not leading from a 3-card suit.
    The 3 can not be the highest card from a worthless 3-card suit. If your partner held a 3-card suit headed Q J, he would lead the Q instead of the 3. He probably would not lead from a 3-card suit headed by 1 honor, unless you had bid the suit.
    Your partner probably is not leading a singleton.
    He would not lead his singleton, unless you had bid a suit.
    Therefore, your partner must be leading from a doubleton. He holds the 3 and 2 of Diamonds.

QUIZ 21 (continued)

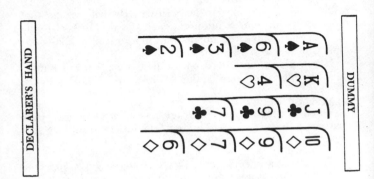

YOUR PARTNER'S HAND

DECLARER'S HAND

DUMMY

YOUR OWN HAND

4. **WHAT DOES YOUR PARTNER'S LEAD TELL YOU?**
   Your opponents' contract is 4 Spades.
   Neither you nor your partner bid.
   Your partner's opening lead is Q of Diamonds.

5. **WHAT DOES YOUR PARTNER'S LEAD TELL YOU?**
   Your opponents' contract is 4 Spades.
   Your partner's opening lead is K of Clubs.

6. **WHAT CARD DO YOU PLAY?**
   Your opponents' contract is 4 Spades.
   Your partner's opening lead is Q of Diamonds.

ANSWERS

4. **YOUR PARTNER HOLDS THE Q J x OF DIAMONDS**
   Your partner probably is not leading a singleton. He would seldom lead a singleton (especially a singleton Q) unless you had bid a suit, which would indicate that you might have a quick entry in that suit.

   Your partner probably is not leading from a doubleton headed by the Q. He would not lead from a high doubleton, unless you had bid the suit.

   Therefore, your partners' lead of an honor indicates that he holds the next lower card, the J, and at least 1 low Diamond.

5. **YOUR PARTNER HOLDS EITHER THE A OR Q OF CLUBS**
   Your partner would not lead the K, unless he held either the A or the Q. The K is led from a suit headed either A K or K Q.

6. **PLAY 8 OF DIAMONDS**
   You want your partner to lead Diamonds again. Therefore, to give him an encouraging "come-on" signal, play a high card instead of your lowest card.

146

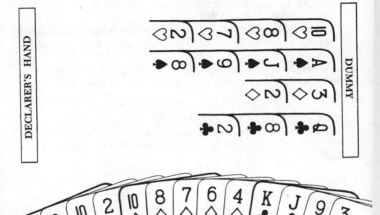

1. **WHAT CARD DO YOU PLAY?**
   Your opponents' contract is 1 No trump.
   Your partner's opening lead is the K of Hearts.

2. **WHAT CARD DO YOU PLAY?**
   Your opponents' contract is 1 No trump.
   Your partner's opening lead is 7 of Clubs.
   Dummy plays the 8 of Clubs.

3. **WHAT DOES YOUR PARTNER'S LEAD TELL YOU?**
   Your opponents' contract is 1 No trump.
   Neither you nor your partner bid.
   Your partner's opening lead is 7 of Clubs.

ANSWERS

1. **PLAY 4 OF DIAMONDS**
   You want to tell your partner to lead Spades, but you can not afford to do so by discarding the 10 of Spades, because the 10 may take a trick.
   If you discard first a low Diamond and then a low Club, you discourage the lead of these 2 suits and invite the lead of a Spade by the process of elimination.

2. **PLAY J OF CLUBS**
   When you play the J of Clubs you tell your partner that you do not hold the 10 of Clubs, because you have played the lowest card in your hand which will serve your purpose.
   When you play the J, you do not deny that you hold the K, because (with the Q in the dummy) declarer must play the A to cover either the J or the K.

3. **YOUR PARTNER PROBABLY IS LEADING HIS HIGHEST CARD FROM A 3-CARD SUIT**
   Your partner is not leading 4th best.
   When you subtract 7 from 11 you get 4. If your partner's lead were fourth best there would be only 4 cards higher than the 7 outside your partner's hand. In your hand and the dummy you can count 5 cards higher than the 7.
   Your partner probably is not leading low from a 3-card suit headed 1 honor or 2 honors not in sequence.
   He would seldom make such a lead, unless you had bid that suit.
   Your partner probably is not leading from a doubleton.
   Against a No trump contract he would avoid a doubleton lead if possible.
   Your partner certainly is not leading a singleton.
   Against a No trump contract he would never lead a singleton, unless you had bid that suit.
   Against a No trump contract the lead of an intermediate card usually indicates the highest card from a worthless 3-card suit.

QUIZ 22 (continued)

YOUR PARTNER'S HAND

DECLARER'S HAND

DUMMY

YOUR OWN HAND

4. **WHAT DOES YOUR PARTNER'S LEAD TELL YOU?**
   Your opponents' contract is 1 No trump.
   Neither you nor your partner bid.
   Your partner's opening lead is 5 of Diamonds.

5. **WHAT DOES YOUR PARTNER'S LEAD TELL YOU?**
   Your opponents' contract is 4 Hearts.
   Your partner's opening lead is A of Diamonds.

6. **WHAT CARD DO YOU PLAY?**
   Your opponents' contract is 4 Hearts.
   Your partner's opening lead is A of Clubs.

ANSWERS

4. **PARTNER IS LEADING FOURTH BEST FROM 4-CARD SUIT**
   Your partner certainly is not leading a singleton.
   Against a No trump contract he would never lead a singleton unless you had bid the suit.
   **Your partner can not be leading his highest card from a
   3-card suit or a doubleton.** Because in your hand and the
   dummy you can see the 2, 3, and 4 of Diamonds, you know
   your partner's 5 is the lowest card in his suit.
   **Your partner probably is not leading low from a 3-card
   suit.** He would seldom lead from a 3-card suit headed by
   1 honor or 2 honors not in sequence, unless you had bid
   the suit. If he held a 3-card suit headed by 2 honors in sequence, he would lead the highest of the 2 honors.
   Your partner is probably leading fourth best.
   By subtracting 5 from 11 you know that there are 6 cards
   higher than the 5 outside your partner's hand. In your hand
   and the dummy you can count only 4 of these cards. Declarer must hold 2 cards higher than the 5.

5. **YOUR PARTNER DOES NOT HOLD THE K OF DIAMONDS**
   Against a trump contract the K is led from a suit headed A K, unless the suit is an A K doubleton. **So the lead
   of the A denies that the K is held,** unless your partner follows up immediately by leading the K.

6. **PLAY THE 9 OF CLUBS**
   Since you want your partner to lead Clubs again, play a
   high Club, not your lowest. **A high card requests your partner to continue leading Clubs.**

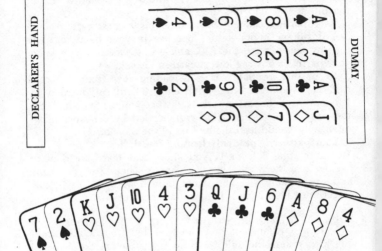

YOUR PARTNER'S HAND

DECLARER'S HAND

DUMMY

YOUR OWN HAND

1. **WHAT CARD DO YOU PLAY?**
   Your opponents' contract is 4 Spades.
   Your partner's opening lead is K of Diamonds.

2. **WHAT DOES YOUR PARTNER'S LEAD TELL YOU?**
   Your opponents' contract is 4 Spades.
   You opened the bidding with 1 Heart.
   Your partner raised your Hearts.
   Your partner's opening lead is the 8 of Hearts.

3. **WHAT DOES YOUR PARTNER'S LEAD TELL YOU?**
   Your opponents' contract is 3 No trump.
   Neither you nor your partner bid.
   Your partner's opening lead is the J of Spades.

ANSWERS

1. **PLAY 8 OF DIAMONDS**
    When you follow suit with a higher card than necessary,
you give your partner a "come-on" signal suggesting that he
should lead that suit again.

2. **YOUR PARTNER IS LEADING FROM A 3-CARD SUIT HEADED
   BY THE Q**
    Your partner is not leading fourth best.
    When you subtract 8 from 11 you get 3. If your partner's
lead were 4th best there would be only 3 cards higher than
the 8 outside your partner's hand. You can count 3 higher
cards in your own hand. If your partner held the A, he
would have led the A instead of the 8 against a trump contract. Therefore, the A must be in declarer's hand. So you
know that there are at least 4 cards higher than the 8 not
in your partner's hand.
    **Your partner is not leading from a worthless 3-card suit,
a doubleton, or a singleton.**
    Your partner raised your Hearts, so you know he has ade-
quate trump support. Three small trumps are not adequate
support, nor is a doubleton or singleton.
    **Your partner is leading low from a 3-card suit headed by
the Q.**
    Since your partner does not have a 4-card or longer Heart
suit but still has adequate trump support, he must hold 3
Hearts headed by the Q. If he held the A, he would have
led the A instead of the 8 against a trump contract.

3. **YOUR PARTNER HOLDS THE 10 OF SPADES. HE DOES NOT
   HOLD THE Q OF SPADES.**
    Against a No trump contract your partner would not lead
a singleton, or from a doubleton headed by the J, unless you
had bid the suit. Therefore, your partner's lead of an honor
denies that he holds the next higher honor (the Q) and indicates that he does hold the next lower card (the 10), and
probably only 1 other low Spade. If your partner held the
J 10 x x, he would lead fourth best against a No trump contract. He might possibly be leading from an intermediate sequence K J 10, or from a solid sequence J 10 9.

QUIZ 24

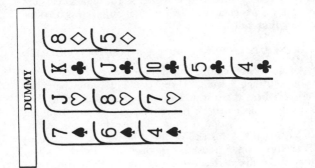

YOUR PARTNER'S HAND

DUMMY

DECLARER'S HAND

YOUR OWN HAND

1. **WHAT CARD DO YOU PLAY?**
   Your opponents' contract is 2 Spades.
   Your opening lead was A of Hearts.
   Your partner did not follow suit.
   What card will you lead now?

2. **WHAT CARD DO YOU PLAY?**
   Your opponents' contract is 1 No trump.
   When declarer leads the Q of Clubs, what card will you play?

3. **WHAT DOES YOUR PARTNER TELL YOU?**
   Your opponents' contract is 2 Spades.
   Your opening lead is the A of Hearts.
   Your partner follows suit with the 6 of Hearts.

ANSWERS

1. **LEAD 10 OF HEARTS**

   Your partner will trump your next lead of Hearts. If he knows which suit to lead in order to throw the lead back into your hand again, he can probably trump a second Heart. There are obviously only 2 suits through which he can hope to put you back in the lead — Diamonds and Clubs.

   If you now lead the 10 of Hearts (a high card) you tell him to lead back the higher ranking of these 2 suits, which is Diamonds.

2. **PLAY THE 8 OF CLUBS FIRST AND THE 2 OF CLUBS NEXT**

   Dummy holds a long, strong Club suit, but no reentries in other suits. If your partner holds the A and 2 small Clubs, he does not want to play the A so long as the declarer can still lead Clubs.

   If you play first high then low, you tell your partner that you do not hold exactly 3 Clubs. Your partner will recognize that the 2 must be your last Club, for the following reason. With 5 Clubs originally in the dummy and 3 in your partner's hand, your partner will know (when declarer leads his second Club and you follow with the 2) that you could not have been dealt 4 Clubs.

   Therefore, your partner will know that declarer still has a third Club, so he will not play his A on the second Club trick.

3. **YOUR PARTNER HOLDS THE K OF HEARTS**

   Considering the Hearts in your own hand and those exposed in the dummy, it is reasonable to assume that the 6 is not the lowest Heart your partner holds. When your partner plays an unnecessarily high Heart (not his lowest Heart), he invites you to lead the suit again. He would not want a second lead of Hearts, unless he held the K.

PART IV

SUMMARY

SUMMARY

OPENING LEADS

THE SUIT TO LEAD AGAINST A NO TRUMP CONTRACT

ATTACKING LEADS

Lead longest and strongest suit in combined hands.
Prefer partner's suit to your own, unless you have:
1. Suit you bid and partner raised.
2. Singleton in partner's suit and a strong suit of your own.
3. Long solid suit and enough entries to set contract unaided.

PROTECTING LEADS

Lead worthless 4-card suit.
Lead worthless 3-card suit.
Lead 3-card suit headed by 2 honors in sequence.
Lead low doubleton.

WHEN PARTNER DOUBLES

If partner bid, lead partner's suit.
If you bid and partner did not bid, lead suit you bid.
If neither you nor partner bid, lead suit dummy bid, unless dummy rebid
or declarer raised that suit.

THE SUIT TO LEAD AGAINST A TRUMP CONTRACT

ATTACKING LEADS

Lead suit you bid and partner raised.
Lead partner's suit.
Lead suit headed A K, solid sequence, or interrupted sequence.
With 4 or more trumps, lead same suit as against No trump.

PROTECTING LEADS

Lead low doubleton.
Lead worthless 3-card suit.
Lead worthless 4-card suit.
Lead trumps, if you hold 2 or 3 small trumps.

GOOD RUFFING LEADS

All 3 of the following requirements are necessary.
1. Your partner has bid.
2. You hold a stopper in trumps.
3. You hold at least 1 "extra" trump.

THE CARD TO LEAD

WHEN LEADING AN HONOR

From touching honors lead highest honor in sequence.
Exception Lead K from suit headed A K.

FROM A DOUBLETON

Lead highest card.

FROM 3-CARD SUIT

Lead highest card, as a general rule.
Lead low from suit headed 1 honor or 2 honors not in sequence.
Exception Lead A against trump contract.

FROM 4-CARD OR LONGER SUIT

Lead fourth best, as a general rule.

Lead an honor instead of fourth best from the following suits:

Against trump contract
Any suit headed .... A, or 2 honors in sequence, or a leadable sequence.

Against No trump
Partner's suit headed .... 2 honors in sequence, or a leadable sequence.
Suit not partner's headed .... a leadable sequence.

LEADS AGAINST SLAMS

ATTACKING LEADS

Lead an A, or lead to establish a second round winner,
  but only with a probable re-entry in your own or partner's hand.
Avoid attacking leads against 6 No trump or any grand slam.

PROTECTING LEADS

Lead same as against mere game contract.
Usually avoid a trump lead.

DESPERATION LEADS

Lead a singleton, even without requirements for good ruffing lead.
Lead low from a suit containing a lone K or Q.
Avoid a desperation lead against 6 No trump or any grand slam.

WHEN PARTNER DOUBLES A SLAM CONTRACT

Make an unusual lead.

LEADABLE SEQUENCES

SOLID SEQUENCES
A K Q, K Q J, Q J 10, J 10 9, 10 9 8.

INTERRUPTED SEQUENCES
A K J, K Q 10, Q J 9, J 10 8, 10 9 7.

INTERMEDIATE SEQUENCES
A Q J, A J 10, A 10 9, K J 10, K 10 9, Q 10 9.

SIGNALS

LEAD-DIRECTING SIGNALS

WHEN PARTNER DOUBLES A 3 NO TRUMP CONTRACT

If your partner bid, lead your partner's suit.
If you bid and your partner did not bid, lead suit you bid.
If neither you nor partner bid, lead suit dummy bid unless dummy rebid or declarer raised that suit.

WHEN PARTNER DOUBLES A RESPONSE TO BLACKWOOD

Lead the suit your partner has doubled.

WHEN PARTNER DOUBLES A SLAM CONTRACT

Make an unusual lead

WHEN PARTNER ALLOWS YOUR TAKEOUT DOUBLE TO STAND

Lead trumps unless you have a strong attacking lead.

INFORMATION GIVEN BY OPENING LEAD

LEAD OF HONOR CARD

Usually denies the next higher card.
Usually guarantees next lower card.

LEAD OF ACE AGAINST NO TRUMP

Shows long solid suit.
Tells partner to unblock.

LEAD OF CARD OTHER THAN AN HONOR

Against trump contract − − Usually shows doubleton, or top of 3 cards.
Against No trump contract − Usually shows fourth best, or top of 3 cards.

WHEN FOLLOWING SUIT OR DISCARDING

WHEN YOU ARE TRYING TO WIN TRICK

Play of any card denies a lower card serving same purpose.

WHEN YOU ARE NOT TRYING TO WIN TRICK

To discourage lead of suit − Play low, or first low then high.
To encourage lead of suit − Play high, or first high then low.

WHEN DUMMY HOLDS LONG SUIT, BUT NO OTHER ENTRIES

To let partner know when to play his stopper:
If you hold exactly 3 cards − Play first low then high in that suit.
If you hold 2 cards or 4 cards − Play first high then low in that suit.

WHEN PLAYING A TRUMP

If you have 3 trumps, and
If you can and want to ruff some suit
Follow suit first high then low.
If you have 3 trumps
Ruff first high then low.

SUIT-PREFERENCE SIGNAL

When signal cannot be mistaken
When obviously partner must select lead from 1 of 2 suits only.

Play unnecessarily high card to suggest lead of higher ranking suit.
Play lowest card − to suggest lead of lower ranking suit.